SORT YOUR
SH*T OUT

Published in 2020 by Welbeck
An imprint of the Welbeck Publishing Group
20 Mortimer Street
London W1T 3JW

Text © Caroline Jones 2020
Design © Welbeck 2020

A CIP catalogue for this book is available from the
British Library.

ISBN 978-1-78739-349-3

10 9 8 7 6 5 4 3 2

SORT YOUR SH*T OUT

EASY STEPS TO A TIDY HOME, MIND AND LIFE

CAROLINE JONES

WELBECK

CONTENTS

SECTION TWO – SORT YOUR SH*T ON THE OUTSIDE: HOME & WORK

SECTION THREE: JOURNALLING YOUR WAY OUT OF CLUTTER AND CHAOS

INTRODUCTION

HOW TO BANISH CLUTTER FROM YOUR LIFE FOR GOOD

"Tidy house, tidy mind" goes the saying. So it follows that with an untidy house comes an untidy mind - all of which makes for a more messy and stressful way of living.

Indeed, if you're seeking true happiness, you really do need to sort your shit out, plain and simple.

It might seem a stretch to equate a more streamlined home with inner peace, but study after study has linked both physical and emotional decluttering with a greater sense of success and satisfaction with life.

It turns out that all the excess things we keep with us, both internally and externally, can have a profound impact on our current wellbeing - and our future emotional life.

Clutter in our physical environment and relationships can keep us rooted in the past, and blocks the flow of positive energy and forward momentum.

Just think about it for a moment. When we have too much junk and unwanted stuff in our lives, there simply isn't space for all those good things to enter - the more spiritually nourishing experiences that most of us thirst for. We all want more fulfilling relationships, greater success in our chosen field, clothes we love and a home we find beautiful, yet most of us crowd out the necessary spaces with an excess of mediocre, unused rubbish that adds little to our lives.

And while many of us view decluttering as simply the clearing out of our physical world, it's just as important that we sweep aside all the unnecessary mental and emotional debris from our interior world as well.

"HAPPINESS IS FINDING THE PERFECT BALANCE BETWEEN TOO LITTLE AND TOO MUCH."

It's an unfortunate part of the human condition to hold onto resentment, anger and disappointment, often for years after the initial act that caused these feelings. Yet by refusing to let go of these negative emotions, it becomes difficult to allow gratitude in and feel full appreciation for the many good things in our life right now.

The relationship between physical mess and emotional mess also supports a more holistic view of sorting your shit out. Research has proven that excess clutter has been shown to trigger stress, fatigue and depression. One study by the University of Southern California found that levels of the stress hormone cortisol were higher in those who lived in homes they described as "cluttered" or full of "unfinished projects".

On the flip side, decluttering has been shown to help boost overall productivity. This is because an overcrowded space is visually distracting and can affect your ability to concentrate on one thing at a time - even if you think you're multi-tasking efficiently. According to a study by the Princeton Neuroscience Institute, clutter overloads the visual cortex and interferes with its ability to process information.

What this means is that when you have a clear out, you're able to think and work more efficiently, enabling you to spend less time on tasks both at home and at work. In turn, this will leave you with more time to enjoy the good stuff in life, such as spending time with family and friends and pursuing hobbies and leisure time.

Not only that, the relationship between physical mess and emotional stress is so strong that living with too much clutter can trigger poor food choices and ultimately lead to weight gain. One study conducted by researchers at Florida State University uncovered a link between hoarding and obesity, noting that people with extremely cluttered homes were 77 per cent more likely to be overweight.

Of course, not everybody's home falls into the excessive-hoarding category, but some experts believe that even milder clutter habits could point to a general picture of being too busy and frazzled to either clear up or eat well. We do know that when people are in a hurry, they're more likely to eat what's handy, grabbing pre-packaged and fast foods, which in turn can lead to obesity. In a more organized home, there's more time and space to plan and prepare healthier meals – as well as the opportunity to sit down at a table and eat more slowly and mindfully, both of which have been shown by countless studies to reduce the number of calories we consume in one sitting.

Put simply, unless your kitchen is organized to encourage home cooking, the chances of you actually making that healthy meal rather than ordering another takeaway decrease rapidly.

And the relationship between physical stuff and mental wellbeing does not stop there. Simply letting go of unnecessary possessions can help you let go of unhelpful mental junk from the past. Just spending time sifting through all the personal items you've gathered over the years can be an emotional rollercoaster, stirring up long-forgotten memories, good and bad. But on the plus side, this emotional exercise gives you the chance to finally address, and then put to bed, some of those negative feelings that have long held the ability to drag you down. Rationalize the feelings, realize the past doesn't matter anymore, ditch that memento of a bad experience and move on. Live in the here and now.

"A SIMPLER, MORE STREAMLINED LIFE IS NOT JUST SEEING HOW LITTLE WE CAN GET BY WITH, OR HOW MUCH WE CAN THROW OUT, BUT LEARNING TO IDENTIFY AND DITCH THE EXCESS."

This book is here to help you on this important journey – a practical guide to getting rid of any unnecessary physical and psychological baggage that's holding you back.

A simpler, more streamlined life is not just seeing how little we can get by with, or how much we can throw out, but learning to identify and ditch the excess, creating more space for you to use what is truly vital, more efficiently and more joyfully.

As you embark on your decluttering journey, it's easy to become overwhelmed by the scale of the task or your seeming lack of progress unless you have proper support and expert help to make the right changes in the right order. This no-nonsense, positive and interactive book will guide you through the decluttering process, step by step, so you won't feel daunted at the prospect.

The advice here will give you the confidence and the skills to take a step back and assess everything in your life, from your home to your relationships, and determine where the most troublesome clutter has accumulated – and how to ditch it.

When you're clear about your personal priorities, you can painlessly discard whatever doesn't support this sense of purpose, whether it's clutter in your cupboards or commitments on your calendar. And once you start to get rid of the unnecessary physical and psychological baggage that is cluttering your days and disturbing your nights, your life will immediately change for the better. By following some of the proven journalling and life coaching techniques in this book, you'll be walked through each key step of sorting your shit out – and will come out the other side of this liberating process richer in time and money, more organized, more driven and clearer-headed than ever before.

So what are you waiting for? Read on for step one...

SECTION ONE

SORT YOUR SH*T ON THE INSIDE: EMOTION & MIND CONTROL

DECLUTTER YOUR MIND

The first space to target in your search for a more ordered life is between the ears. Just like our cupboards and cellars, our minds need a thorough sort through from time to time. Of course, we all hold emotional baggage – storing sentiment and strong feelings is part of life's rich journey. But problems can occur when we keep adding more unprocessed memories to our already over-stuffed emotional bags, never letting anything go, holding on to every new insult, hurt feeling and angry thought.

Emotional hoarders are a bit like shopaholics who never get rid of anything – they just keep on buying new things without getting rid of all the old, broken, worn-out stuff, and before long, their house becomes out of control, untidy and messy.

In the same way, if we don't declutter our mind and let go of those unwanted, painful emotions, then no matter how much we try to fill our mind with life's more wonderful feelings such as joy, happiness and gratitude, there just won't be enough room. The good will become tarnished by the bad.

Emotions, like any physical junk accumulation, need to be actively decluttered – and on a regular basis. Otherwise the negative ones have a habit of just piling up, one after another to make us feel more and more miserable.

Getting rid of all this non-essential mental baggage is therefore crucial to staying focused, motivated and productive in our daily life.

Research does show that physically clearing out those untidy cupboards and rooms does have positive mental health benefits

– and that's what we'll be focusing on in the second half of this book. But before you start grabbing boxes, we're going to spend some time clearing out inner clutter, directly addressing untidy emotions to help us live a happier, freer, more peaceful life. Getting rid of all the junk we no longer want to use but which sits in our hearts gathering dust and causing problems.

Bottling up your emotions can leave you feeling stuck in the past. But by sorting through these feelings, you can redirect that misplaced energy into moving forward to a more positive life.

When emotions are suppressed, anxiety and depression can often follow, so it's essential to clean up your thoughts for a fresh start. However, that's not to say this first step will be easy. Unlike physical clutter, emotional clutter can be extremely difficult to let go of – we can't just pile it all into black bin bags and head down to the thrift or charity shop. Not least because no one else wants your emotional clutter – they each have plenty of their own!

The key to decluttering sentimental junk is moving from suppression to expression. To let go of any emotion, it needs to be properly expressed, to be felt fully first before it can be forgotten. Ugly, hurtful memories and personal grudges need to be out in the open and perhaps even shared with the other people they involve. In theory, this all sounds simple enough but in practice, of course, expressing painful emotions is much harder.

Sometimes it becomes difficult to reach out, to let yourself be vulnerable, to say what's really bothering you. But try to think of issues left undealt with as stuck energy that holds us back from living a happier, more fulfilled life. The more we work on ourselves, the more we allow ourselves to feel then let go of unwanted negative emotions, and the more energy we have to create the lives we want. This trick is called "emotional decluttering" and, once mastered, it will become a great way to clear and rebalance your mind for the rest of your life.

Here's how to get started...

"FREE YOUR MIND FROM CLUTTER, AND SUDDENLY CLEARING THE JUNK FROM THE REST OF YOUR LIFE FEELS ACHIEVABLE."

VISUALIZE HOW YOU WANT YOUR LIFE TO LOOK

Spend the next few minutes thinking about your ideal life.
Would it involve a career change, meeting a life partner,
doing something positive for your family or for society, even?
By imagining your dream destination, you can start to think
about all the small steps it takes to get there.

THREE THINGS I'D LOVE TO HAPPEN IN MY LIFE

1) ....

....

....

....

2) ....

....

....

....

3) ....

....

....

....

Now write out what your life currently looks like in the same three areas – add lots of details. Pay close attention to your true feelings about all these aspects and how that impacts your desire for change. For example, if you want to focus on your love life, but you know you haven't got over your ex yet, this is an area you'll need to release some negative emotion around.

MY LIFE RIGHT NOW...

1) ....
....
....
....

2) ....
....
....
....

3) ....
....
....
....

WRITE DOWN WHAT'S HOLDING YOU BACK

Following the same process, note down all the situations or areas you think you need to address to help get you to where you would like to be. There are no wrong answers here. These are the things you believe are blocking or limiting you.

Is it the way your best never seemed to be good enough for one parent? Or has a partner made you feel undervalued while you were together? Drill into the details.

And be honest with yourself. This step is essential to declutter your emotions. For this you'll have to dig deep and uncover the old patterns you are still stuck in. Putting them in writing helps you to have a clear vision of the overall picture and identify the work that needs to be done to move forward.

WHAT'S BLOCKING OR LIMITING ME...

1) ....

....

2) ....

....

3) ....

....

....

TAKE A TRIP DOWN MEMORY LANE

It won't be easy at first, but spend some time revisiting each of the scenarios that are holding you back and try to pinpoint their root cause. This will help you to feel the raw emotion and understand what might be limiting you from moving forward.

Whether it's about an ex-partner who pulled away or an old boss who got uncomfortably close, make yourself think about that person and how they made you feel. Often we hold our feelings in and choose to distract ourselves from them with food, alcohol or anything that can numb the pain. The trick here is to release the locked emotion. It might hurt for a moment, but you'll feel so much better for releasing it.

As you address each emotion and allow yourself to feel it, you're doing some important mind detoxing. This will allow you to push away these mental blocks and limits with a virtual broom. Just put pen to paper and write down all the feelings that come up for each memory. Again, there are no wrong answers when it comes to your emotions. Once this is done, you can start to address what needs to happen to help you feel differently. Come up with a simple point of action for each area of memory.

THE MEMORIES HOLDING ME BACK:

1) ....

2) ....

3) ....

MY ACTION PLAN TO MOVE ON:

1) ....

....

....

....

....

2) ....

....

....

....

....

3) ....

....

....

....

....

....

....

REWRITE YOUR STORY

Now you've addressed emotions that are holding you back, take the time to write the new, improved story of how you want your life to look - the things you want to happen. Really go into detail this time, including a description of what you imagine feeling about each life event as it happens.

MY NEW STORY

1) ....

....

....

....

2) ....

....

....

....

3) ....

....

....

NOW, GO MAKE IT HAPPEN

Write down a few simple first steps you can implement to begin
your new story and make your journey toward it a reality.
It doesn't matter how small these first steps might seem, just
working on the story every day will breed your belief in it. Be
confident but realistic, and be nice to yourself along the way.
It may take time and there could be setbacks and stumbles, but
you will get there in the end.

MY FIRST STEPS

1) ....

....

....

2) ....

....

....

3) ....

....

....

....

....

NOTES

FIVE WAYS TO LIVE A LESS CLUTTERED EMOTIONAL LIFE

1. LET GO OF ANGER

Many of us have a forgotten shelf somewhere that's crammed with too many pictures and knick-knacks to count, a messy spot that's a magnet for attracting dust and dirt in hard-to-reach areas. As a result, we can never face the thought of cleaning the shelf and so actively avoid it, letting the cobwebs build up over years.

Anger can work in the same way, with each rage-inducing event accumulating inside us over time, until the very idea of dealing with the source feels too overwhelming. But if built-up anger and resentment are getting in the way of your life, it's time to do something about it. A good place to start is to stop expecting people to be perfect and to stop taking their flaws and mistakes as a personal insult.

If someone has an annoying habit that enrages you every time it happens (perhaps out of all proportion) then maybe let them off the hook - and yourself too. Try to let daily life happen without judgement and realize that most people are doing the best they can - just like you. This approach will help anger to dissipate and allow more compassionate feelings to grow instead.

"TRY TO LET DAILY LIFE HAPPEN WITHOUT JUDGEMENT AND REALIZE THAT MOST PEOPLE ARE DOING THE BEST THEY CAN, JUST LIKE YOU."

2. STOP HOLDING GRUDGES

When something hurts us, evolutionary instinct encourages us to hang onto the pain to make sure we don't forget and can never be hurt in the same way again. But while that instinct remains useful for teaching children about danger, it's not a good way for fully grown adults to handle emotional relationships. Constantly looking backward keeps you standing still - or crashing into obstacles on the path in front of you. Instead of holding on, let go of the need to punish and try to forgive and move past it. You can't change the past - only the way you respond to it. Forgive for your own sake only, if not for the person who upset you in the first place.

Keeping baggage from the past will leave no room for happiness in the future.

3. DON'T LET ENVY RULE

Envious emotions can seriously clutter our heart and minds
if they're allowed free rein. In this era of social media over-
sharing, it's a constant battle. We experience envy over other
people's appearance, talents, relationships and lifestyles.
Yet these feelings provide no positive contribution to our
lives. So it's time to break free. Remind yourself that nobody
has it all. Comparing your life with others is always a
losing proposition.

There will always appear to be people who have it better than
you. At least on the surface. So if social media sucks you into
an envy cycle then perhaps it's time to cut down your usage or
even close your account. And remember, we always compare the
worst of what we know about ourselves to the best assumptions
we make about others. Be reminded, despite what Instagram might
suggest, that nobody has the perfect life. Each person you meet
in real life experiences problems, trials and weaknesses just
like you. This is what makes us human.

4. LIVE WITH LESS FEAR

Fear is another area of emotional clutter we often haul around with us unnecessarily. It's not possible to completely eliminate fear - and it's a useful instinct when it comes to sensing real danger. But the key is not to let any fear based on past experiences control you and stop you doing the things you want to do in life.

This is particularly true when those fears are not rational. For example, just because you were made redundant in your last job, it doesn't mean it will happen again in your new role. Rationalize your fears and list all the logical reasons why the outcome you're most worried about is actually very unlikely to happen.

What am I afraid of?	Why is this unlikely to happen?
1.	
2.	
3.	
4.	
5.	

5. TRAIN YOURSELF TO BE AN OPTIMIST

Seeing life as a glass half empty and always expecting the worst is one of the easiest but most damaging ways to fill our minds with emotional clutter that gets in the way of enjoying daily life. Think about how you bag up old clothes to give them away and try adopting the same approach to negative thinking - just give it all away. Don't hold onto such useless thoughts for another moment.

Pessimists often end up missing enriching life experiences and pushing other people away. Studies have even shown they don't live as long as optimists. So, make a conscious decision to hope for the best in all situations - and aim to find a silver lining even when things do fall short of your expectations.

Positive thinking is more than just a tagline - it changes the way we behave.

OTHER WAYS TO FREE UP SOME HEADSPACE

Do you feel like a constant stream of clutter is turning your brain into a spaghetti junction? Streamline your mind and bring calm to the chaos with some of these tips…

KEEP TWO DIARIES

Have one journal for writing down all the good stuff – jotting down all the nice things that have happened and recording all the good feelings and your gratitude for them. Then keep another as an outlet for any negative crap. Think of it as a place to dump all the bad stuff: your anger, your frustrations, your fears and insecurities. Getting it all out on paper will lift a huge weight from you, so you'll feel free and lighter.

But – and this is important – just as you wouldn't keep lifting the lid on the trash to check what's inside, don't be tempted go back and read over your negative thoughts once you have offloaded them. This will only result in you reliving them and feeling bad again, which defeats the object of having ditched them in the first place! On the other hand, do get in the habit of regularly rereading your happiness journal as going back over beautiful memories will boost your mood and encourage healthy feelings of thankfulness.

SET PRIORITIES

Prioritizing is a great way to proactively take charge of your future and stop life's noise holding you back. The first step is to figure out what the things are that matter the most to you, your life aspirations and your long-term goals. Write a list of your top priorities and make sure that the actions and decisions you take always reflect them. Next, create an action plan to meet those goals and to work on how you want to divide your time to focus on each item on that list.

MY LIFE ASPIRATIONS

ACTION PLAN

	ACTIONS
SHORT—TERM GOALS	
LONG—TERM GOALS	

DEADLINE	RESULT

QUIETEN THE CHATTER

At any given time of day our minds are cluttered with a constant background of chatter that controls how we think and feel. It keeps us from being present in the moment.

Staying in the moment can be really challenging, especially when our mind keeps on dragging us to places we don't want to go. For example, we might be trying to enjoy a sunny holiday abroad, but our mind keeps on chattering about the work we left behind. Or we're too busy wondering whether people will like our holiday photos on social media to actually enjoy the beautiful scenery.

Practising regular meditation is one of the best ways to train yourself to be wholeheartedly in the moment. But just like any other skill worth acquiring, mindfulness requires a lot of practice. Downloading an app on to your smartphone, such as Calm, is a great way to get started. And remember, being mindful doesn't have to involve sitting cross-legged, closing your eyes and chanting mantras. Meditation can be done in any place, at any time.

Just breathing in and out, counting slowly to five for the inhale and five again for the exhale can be enough to help tune out the mental chatter and get your mind back on track.

AVOID MULTI-TASKING

It may sound counter-productive, but splitting your attention often means nothing gets done properly. So, typing up that work report while checking your Facebook feed and helping your kids with their homework does nobody any favours. Constant juggling between tasks limits your attention span, increases stress and creates additional clutter by making it difficult for your brain to filter out irrelevant information.

Indeed, one study by Stanford University showed that heavy multi-tasking lowers efficiency and may even impair your brain control. The solution is to single-task as much as possible. Make a list of things you need to get done that day; keep the to-do list simple and realistic. Start with what's most important and work your way down it, one task at a time.

TO DO TODAY (FROM "MUST-DO" TO "MEH"):

....

....

....

....

....

....

....

....

RECLASSIFY BAD EXPERIENCES

Our life stories are the versions of events that we ourselves have created and filed away in our mental library. But whether it's the good or the bad, it's important to remember that our recollections never represent an entirely accurate series of events.

When we say, "This is who I am", what we really mean is, "This is who I think I am based on my memories." We are just narrating the biography we and those around us have written for us. Yet it's part of the human condition to go back and relive dramatic events that were full of sadness, anger, betrayal or fear - and to go on living our life based on these seminal stories we tell ourselves. But despite the addictive drama, these stories create nothing but a clutter of negative emotions in our mind. They just remind us of pain we experienced in the past. Of course, we can't wipe out these memories but what we can do is reclassify them as life lessons. Ask yourself: "Is my memory of this really true, and if it is, what has this experience taught me about life?"

The good news is these stories are fluid, not set in stone, and we have the power to change and re-write them at any time - moving on from the versions that hold us back.

MEMORY	IS THIS REALLY TRUE?	WHAT HAS THIS EXPERIENCE TAUGHT ME?

BE MORE DECISIVE

When you constantly put off making decisions, your brain becomes overwhelmed by the clutter that comes from carrying around all the variables of the decision-making process. So stop procrastinating and decide today. Whether it's about taking a new job, asking out someone you've fancied for ages or clearing out your kitchen cupboards - get it done.

This doesn't mean making rash decisions - it's often still important to carefully evaluate all the pros and cons, but remember, we may never have all the information we need. So make up your mind, do what your heart tells you - and don't look back again.

Three things I want to do but keep putting off:

1) ....
....
....
....

2) ....
....
....
....

3) ....
....
....

Now... go!

"MAKE UP YOUR MIND, DO WHAT YOUR HEART TELLS YOU – AND DON'T LOOK BACK AGAIN."

STOP THE GUILT CYCLE

Irrational guilt often occurs when we are too hard on ourselves and expect everything to be perfect. For example, this might be the nagging feeling that you're a bad parent because you're not feeding your child the right foods, or stimulating their brains enough - or just because you snapped at them once after a long day at work. Equally, you might feel like a bad son or daughter because you don't call your own parents enough. Take a moment to remind yourself that no one gets everything right all of the time, and you shouldn't expect yourself to. Next time those doubts start to pile up in your mind it's important to tell yourself: "I am trying my best and I am enough."

SLASH YOUR USE OF SOCIAL MEDIA

As an increasing amount of psychological research is showing, the social media you consume has a huge impact on your mental health. We now spend hours online: looking at Instagram and Twitter feeds, managing Pinterest boards, watching viral videos on YouTube. But the sheer abundance of information can clog your brain, causing stress and anxiety.

Social media also fuels our need to feel validated and approved constantly. For example, "If my picture only gets five likes, but my friend's post gets fifty likes, that means people like her more than me." No matter how ridiculous this sounds said out loud, it's often how we subconsciously feel. And it can lead to many unhealthy behaviours, such as virtual stalking and constant comparison. Limiting social media usage as much as possible and striving to build real face-to-face relationships is the key to getting rid of this unwanted mental baggage.

You can start by setting a limit on the amount of time you spend on social media. Also, be selective about which services you use - skip any that make you feel bad. And turn off those alerts!

TAKE TIME OUT TO UNWIND

Your brain needs to rest and recharge in order to perform smoothly. So have a nightly screen curfew where you switch off your phones and TVs and do something that makes you feel happy - such as take a bath, read a book or meditate.

AND BREATHE...

Take a deep breath. Pause. Exhale slowly. Repeat five times. How do you feel? Calmer, more in control? Deep breathing is a simple yet effective technique to clear your mind, induce tranquility and elevate your mood instantly. It lowers the heart rate and blood pressure and stimulates the parasympathetic nervous system, which helps your body relax. As well as being a brilliant stress-reliever, breathing exercises also promote concentration and focus.

Don't just be good to others - be good to yourself too!

HOW TO DECLUTTER YOUR FRIENDSHIPS

It might seem a little harsh to talk about decluttering friends just as you would your bathroom cabinet, but in truth, relationships are an area of our lives in which unhealthy baggage can easily accumulate. It's important to stop from time to time and reflect on which people in our social orbit aren't adding value to our life experience - or perhaps are even actively taking something away from it with their negativity.

Research shows we are directly influenced by the people we choose to surround ourselves with. The strong peer effect begins early at school, but remains an important feature throughout our lives. So, if you're striving for success and joy, surrounding yourself with others who also have these traits is extremely important, as they will reflect and amplify your own positivity.

Picking a set of friends who will support us through life's inevitable ups and downs is also critical. Humans are social animals, and making lasting connections to others is important in forming and maintaining a strong sense of self Which is not to stay all friends serve the same purpose in our life - we tend to have a wide range of friends who sit in different categories.

FUNCTIONAL OR FUN FRIEND?

For example, there are functional friendships that offer mutual benefit for a specific reason. They might be with a colleague or another parent at your child's school, for example, or perhaps with a neighbour whose cats you feed and houses you check on when you each go on holiday.

" IF YOU'RE STRIVING FOR SUCCESS AND JOY, SURROUNDING YOURSELF WITH OTHERS WHO ALSO HAVE THESE TRAITS IS EXTREMELY IMPORTANT, AS THEY WILL REFLECT AND AMPLIFY YOUR OWN POSITIVITY. "

Then there are friendships based more on pleasure and fun, the type of relationship which exists between people who enjoy a shared interest - be it members of the same sports team or of a book club, or regulars in a yoga class.

Both functional and purely fun-based friendships tend to end when your life circumstances change. The former come to a natural end when the relationship is no longer beneficial to one or both of you - for example, when you leave work or you move house. Likewise, friendships based purely on fun often stop when the thing you have in common comes to an end - you leave the sports team or club or stop going to the gym. Emotionally, it doesn't tend to be a big deal for either person when these more transactional friendships end.

A STRONGER BOND

Then there is the much deeper and less superficial type of friendship - one that's based on mutual respect and shared experiences. These friendships take more time to establish than fun or functional relationships, but they're also stronger and more enduring. They often arise when two people recognize that they have similar values and goals in life, a shared vision for the future. Because they take time to develop and are associated with personal development, they often begin when you are young - at school, university or perhaps in your first job. But deeper bonds can still form later in life too, especially if you remain open to them.

At their best, these friends enrich our lives and we enjoy some of our most meaningful times together. However, because the bond runs deep and the course of the friendship is long, these kinds of relationships can experience lows, too - and at their very worst they can also be a source of great pain.

WHEN TO MOVE ON

While we hope most of the connections we make in life remain close and fulfilling for years, there are some relationships that you know deep down aren't working anymore. Perhaps you struggle to find much in common to talk about, or you've noticed that over time you have developed different values, mindsets or interests. Often changes in careers or moving into different life stages at different times can drive a wedge into a friendship that was forged when you were both young.

It's important to acknowledge that not all friendships are meant to last a lifetime - and that's okay. People move through life at different paces, heading for different destinations. Holding on to people even when a connection turns sour can end up draining your energy and can even stunt your own personal growth.

While we can all probably acknowledge this general truth, it's more difficult to recognize when it's happening to you. If a once-strong friendship is becoming fractious and fractures are starting to appear, the normal instinct is to hang on and hope for repairs. We may get in a cycle of argument and apology, but we tend to ignore the root cause and refuse to recognize that it might be time to let the friendship die.

Indeed, it can be incredibly tough to know when to dig deep and when to let go. For example, if you've been supporting a friend who is struggling with some form of addiction over a long period, at what point do you start to think about the negative impact the cycle of good intentions followed by relapse is causing in your own life?

But the wedges between friends don't have to be as dramatic as lapsed sobriety. For instance, what happens when you realize a friend holds an opinion about something important that is fundamentally different from your own? Perhaps they support a politican that you can't stand. Is it just a minor quirk or a philosophical chasm not worth overcoming?

SHOULD I STAY OR GO?

When differences and challenges arise, it is of course natural to tell yourself that you don't want to be a fair-weather friend and that friendship isn't all about fun, it's about being there for each other through thick and thin.

But while friendships do have natural ups and downs as life events take their toll, if the downs become too extreme or too frequent, it's probably time for a rethink. After all, friends are supposed to be there for the sticky patches in life, not to cause them.

And yet, all too often we stay in damaging relationships from a sense of misplaced loyalty. We treat long-time friends like family – people we owe a duty to, not people we can choose to disconnect from. We feel guilty that, by letting go, we're being not just a bad friend but a bad person. But if you don't have much in common anymore, and if the little time you spend together also makes you feel miserable, then it really is okay to let that friendship go.

Even if you have made a decision to dial down a friendship, actively walking away from it can be hard, which is why so many relationships drag on even when you know it is no longer a positive bond. It might be that you find it hard to walk away because you feel you've put so much into the friendship over the years that cutting ties completely would feel like a waste of all that energy and shared history.

"IF YOU HAVE LITTLE IN COMMON ANY MORE, AND IF THE LITTLE TIME YOU SPEND TOGETHER ALSO MAKES YOU FEEL MISERABLE THEN IT REALLY IS OKAY TO LET THAT FRIENDSHIP GO."

But whether it's someone you've known for six months or a mate since the age of five, friendships need sorting out in much the same way as some of the things in your home. Just as old books, clothes and furniture, which you once loved, often need relegating to the past, so too should you view a friendship that is long past its sell-by-date. The relationship has had its moment, served its purpose perhaps, but trying to resuscitate a seriously stalled friendship rarely works and just ties you to the past. You need to live in the present.

If you work hard to cultivate the best friendships in your life, as well as remaining open to new connections, you will maintain a better quality of life. Spending more time with positive influences means you are much more likely to reach your personal goals because the mindset of the people around you shapes your own mindset more than you think. People who motivate you, support you and see the best in you will help drive you toward living your best life. Bad influences only ever do the opposite.

So create a network that consists entirely of supportive friends and positive forces by taking these steps and carefully declutter your relationships…

DO A FRIEND AUDIT

List all your friends and think carefully about each person. Put them into three lists: Keepers, good for now, and problem friends – these last are the ones who are making you miserable and are the group to focus on when decluttering.

DOES THE FRIENDSHIP HAVE A PROBLEM, OR IS THE PROBLEM THE FRIEND?

Just because you put a friend in the "problem" list doesn't mean they are automatically in the discard pile. Generally speaking, there are two reasons why a relationship can turn toxic. A specific problem has arisen, perhaps an argument has occurred that has never been properly cleared up? Or the real problem is the friend.

If the source is a specific problem then it needs to be addressed and some of the advice in the previous chapter about letting go of grudges and not holding on to anger may well apply. You might need to do your bit to move this friendship out of the problem column. It's always a good idea to address specific problems first as this may well break a negative cycle. But if you've tried tackling past mistakes and addressing arguments but the same issues keep popping up faster than you can solve them, like a game of emotional whack-a-mole, then you likely have an altogether different type of problem – and it may be time to rethink the entire relationship.

KEEPERS	GOOD FOR NOW	PROBLEM

TIME TO SAY GOODBYE?

When looking at the people left on the "problem" list after you've separated out the more superficial problems, you should ask yourself: How do these people make me feel?

Are they adding to your life in any meaningful, supportive way? Or are they making you feel miserable or anxious?

Regardless of who they are or how long the history is, if people are a constant source of negativity in your life and add no value, then it's time to fade them out. Only by distancing yourself from these false friends can you create space to let in more supportive and genuine people. You could choose to cut out negative influences straight away, but if that feels too confrontational for you, it's possible to slowly phase people out simply by consistently saying "no" to meet-ups until the message becomes clear.

DON'T LET FOMO HOLD YOU BACK

Once you've identified someone you want to let go of, the fear of missing out may give you pause. Especially if this is someone you've had fun with in the past. You might wonder if they'll go off and do more interesting things without you, if the old gang will somehow get back together. You could also wonder if it would be possible to develop a better friendship in the future.

This perfectly natural impulse comes from an evolutionary instinct - our ancestors had to stick together and avoid being ostracized from the main group to survive. It's also good to ask these questions of yourself and not act rashly. But remember, you are not a pack animal. You probably have other support networks and it really is fine going it alone sometimes if that means ditching something negative.

"IT REALLY IS FINE GOING IT ALONE SOMETIMES IF THAT MEANS DITCHING SOMETHING NEGATIVE."

PUT YOUR EGO ASIDE

Hesitancy about cutting ties with a bad friend is also inextricably linked to our sense of self-esteem. We're programmed to want validation from others, even if it's from people who aren't healthy for us. Counter this by asking, "When did this friend last make me feel good about myself?" If it was a long time ago, or worse still, never, then you have your answer.

The validation you seek will eventually come from other sources, if you create space for it now. While the process can be difficult, it's important to understand that ditching bad friends will help your more promising friendships to develop further - and help you grow stronger as a result. Having people who are consistently supportive will be better for your ego in the long run than begging for compliment crumbs from someone who's withholding.

LEARN TO SPOT THE EARLY SIGNS OF A TRUE FRIEND

The more clearly you can identify the personality traits that have resulted in your deepest and healthiest friendships, the more you will spot them when you meet new people. In general, seek out people you can trust, people who share your core values and seem to have your best interests at heart.

This doesn't mean getting yourself an adoring fan club that never questions you, though! It's important to have friends who can be honest with you and won't sugar-coat the truth when they know it's what you need to hear. But remember, it's a two-way street; make sure you are giving them the best advice with no ulterior motives.

TRUE FRIEND CHECKLIST

- [ ] Shared values
- [ ] Has your best interests at heart
- [ ] Kind
- [ ] Supportive
- [ ] Honest
- [ ] Trustworthy
- [ ] Gives advice without ulterior motives - and without judgement

WHAT ELSE AM I LOOKING FOR FROM MY FRIENDSHIPS?

DON'T BE AFRAID TO LOOK VULNERABLE

Vulnerability is essential to attract more meaningful
relationships into your life. You reflect back what you put
out, so open up, don't hide your true self from others. A good
friend will love you, warts and all. Being honest allows
others to be authentic around you. Never be afraid to talk
about your fears or voice your opinions. If you have a big
dilemma at work or have developed doubts about your partner,
choosing to talk it through with a friend will make the other
person feel they can do the same with you, so you develop a
bond of mutual trust.

PUT THE MOST EFFORT INTO YOUR BEST FRIENDSHIPS

It might sound obvious but we don't always do this, often
spending the most time and energy on those in closest
physical proximity - or those with the most urgent and
demanding needs.

But the regular maintenance of a long relationship is what
allows it to deepen, so make sure you catch up with old friends
face-to-face whenever you can. And use social media
to be social rather than simply follow and like: message them,
share jokes and news items, or find time to FaceTime. This
gentle, easy connection with people who are equally invested
in the minutiae of your daily life will help your real
friendships grow and last the distance.

Look back at your list of friends that you see as Keepers -
why are these friendships so important to you, and what can
you do to nurture and develop these relationships?

FIVE FRIENDS I WANT TO INVEST MORE TIME IN:	THIS FRIENDSHIP IS GREAT! HERE'S WHY.	HOW CAN I NURTURE THIS FRIENDSHIP?

LESS IS MORE

By decluttering your friendships and ditching the most toxic
ones, you'll feel like a load has been lifted, making life feel
lighter and more positive.

We often wrongly assume that we need more of things in
life to be happy, more experiences to find meaning, more
entertainment to banish stress and anxiety. Often the very
opposite is true. By choosing less over more, and prioritizing
quality over quantity, we eliminate sources of unnecessary
worry, complications and tension. One true friend is worth
50 shallow ones.

"Out of clutter find
simplicity. From discord,
find harmony."

- Albert Einstein

"WE OFTEN WRONGLY ASSUME THAT WE NEED MORE OF THINGS IN LIFE TO BE HAPPY..."

SIX TYPES OF FRIENDS YOU DON'T NEED

While we all have our faults, if someone in your life has consistently demonstrated these negative behaviours, then it's probably time to wave goodbye.

THE EMOTIONAL VAMPIRE

These friends do nothing but drain you emotionally, sucking the life and joy out of everyone around them. They're needy, self-obsessed and unable to see anyone's viewpoint but their own. Even if you've known them for years, you need to let go before they drain you dry!

THE MEAN GOSSIP

Do you have a friend who is always saying nasty things about others? Perhaps they even make sarcastic remarks about you whenever you meet. Yes, they can be fun to be around, but if they can sometimes be snide to your face, have you wondered what they're saying about you when your back is turned? Give them the boot!

THE FINANCIAL DRAIN

We're not talking about a friend who has fallen on hard times and is immensely grateful for any help you can give. A financial drain is that person who never buys a round of drinks, the one who always disappears before the end of a group dinner to avoid their share of the bill. Or perhaps someone who is constantly asking to borrow money. Save your bank balance and fade them out.

THE ENVIER

We've all had a friend who can never seem to support you in your success. They can't help but pick holes in your triumphs and look for the downsides at any given opportunity. What's the point in a friend who can't be happy for you? They're a negative drain. Ditch them and move on.

THE BLAMER

They're in trouble at work, again? It's someone else's fault. They're having relationship problems? It's because their partner isn't pulling their weight. You don't feel supported by them? That's because you're too needy! This type of person will never accept that anything is their fault. It's tiring and it's childish. Next!

THE HOT-AND-COLD FRIEND

One day you're their best buddy and they want to spend lots of time with you and hang out. Next week you might as well be a stranger as they leave your texts unanswered and ghost you on social media. You need stability in your friendships, not a roller coaster ride. Time to go cold on them.

FIVE WAYS YOU'LL FEEL BETTER AFTER A FRIENDSHIP DECLUTTER

1. YOUR STRESS LEVELS WILL BE FAR LOWER

Toxic people, who think only about themselves and require a lot of attention, are pure negative energy in your life, causing nothing but stress and anxiety. You can try to argue with them but they'll still want to be right every time. The fact they won't make compromises will upset you, and their narcissism will often make you feel inferior to them. So let go! It's your job to prioritize your happiness and peace of mind, so don't feel bad about removing these sources of stress.

2. YOU WILL HAVE MORE ENERGY

Having too many friends who are always negative or playing the role of the victim requires a lot of your time, attention and energy. Constantly solving other people's problems will sap your spirit dry! Likewise, having a very judgemental friend who always criticizes you is exhausting. Removing this nagging presence from your life means you can live by your own standards rather than trying to seek the approval of others.

3. YOU WILL REACH YOUR GOALS SOONER

Having toxic people in your life prevents you from moving forward - even if you don't realize it at the time. They're a distraction from the successful direction you need to take. Once you remove roadblocks, you will be able to focus on your own needs and goals once more, and find yourself moving back to your own path in life - without unhelpful detours.

4. YOU WILL HAVE SPACE FOR NEW CONNECTIONS

Everything in life is limited. Resources are limited. Time is limited. Space is limited. What you can accomplish within a lifetime is limited. We simply can't have it all!

This is why you have to be very careful about not only what you choose to do, but with whom you choose to do it. You can only maintain a handful of strong relationships at any given time - you just don't have the time, energy or mental focus to handle more. If you're spending your time with lacklustre individuals, you're likely to live a lacklustre life. Once you get the space you crave, don't be afraid to be picky about who you chose to fill it with.

5. YOU WILL HAVE MORE TIME FOR YOU

One of the best things you can do after a friendship declutter is to work on strengthening your relationship with yourself. Learning to love yourself and enjoy your own company is one of the biggest gifts in life - and a lesson we all have to learn if we want to be truly happy.

So enjoy having more me-time daily instead of having to spend hours on the phone or visiting difficult friends. A social declutter should also remove a lot of negative activities from your diary and daily to-do list, freeing up more time for more nourishing activities. Start meditating, doing yoga, reading great books, learning new things, journalling your thoughts and simply spending more time in nature. Self-care is vital and will help you feel renewed.

Now that you've decluttered this area of your life, you will also have the space and energy to think about decluttering the others. In the next part of the book, we'll work on your home.

SECTION TWO

SORT YOUR SH*T ON THE OUTSIDE: HOME & WORK

TAKING THE NEXT STEP

If you've closely worked through the practical steps and advice on decluttering your emotional life in the first half of this book, you should be feeling more focused and in a better place to turn your attention to addressing the physical clutter in your life.

The remainder of this book will focus on physical spaces, but that doesn't mean it won't continue to contribute to your emotional wellbeing. A raft of research has made a strong link between less clutter and lower stress levels. Indeed, all clutter starts between the ears and in the first plan we will be looking at why we accumulate so much stuff - and why we find it so hard to throw away.

Then we will look at the best strategies for dealing with mess and how to tackle each area of your home, room by room.

WHY DO WE COLLECT CLUTTER?

The fact that you're reading this book probably means you feel that clutter has in some way taken over your life. The first thing to understand is you are really not alone! At some point we've all felt overwhelmed by overflowing wardrobes, a kitchen crammed with so much useless stuff it's hard to cook, or a loft full to the brim with junk. And yet, even when stuff is obviously serving no good purpose, we have all experienced that strange sense of inertia that prevents us from just throwing it out. This reluctance is because, as humans, we are actually hardwired to hang onto stuff: preserving resources is an evolutionary throwback to ensure we're not left empty-handed in times of scarcity. But our life today is very different to that of our ancestors'.

We live in a time of plenty, when most people are more likely to have too much rather than too little, yet the habit of hoarding remains part of our brain circuitry.

Indeed, a recent study by Yale School of Medicine found that, for many, letting go is literally painful. Researchers recruited both non-hoarders and hoarders, and then asked them to sort through items such as junk mail and old newspapers. Some of the items belonged to the scientists, but some actually belonged to the participants. Participants had to decide what to keep and what to throw away. While all this was happening, their brain activity was tracked using an MRI scanner.

Unlike non-hoarders, hoarders showed increased activity in two specific areas of the brain when confronted with their own junk. These two areas - the anterior cingulate cortex and the insula - are both involved with psychological pain. The study found that the more a hoarder reported feeling "not right" about throwing something out, the stronger the activity in those pain parts of the brain.

Interestingly, these very same brain regions are responsible for producing overwhelming cravings in smokers or alcoholics who are trying to quit their habit. The stronger the addiction, the stronger the feelings of anxiety and discomfort, and the greater the urge to drink or smoke.

In habitual hoarders it appears that just the idea of throwing stuff away causes the brain to experience a similar distress signal. And as we're all programmed to avoid pain and discomfort, the brain will seek to relieve this anxiety, which means smokers light up a cigarette, drinkers pour a whiskey and hoarders burrow away their junk.

Each time a hoarder hangs onto something, they seem to feel safer and calmer – and this sense of relief can become addictive.

We know that people with a tendency to hoard feel an irrational conviction that something seemingly old and useless could still have potential value one day in the future. The very idea that they might be throwing away something that could yet be of use becomes painful. And when it comes to something with some sentimental value attached, the urge to keep it forever is even stronger.

You don't have to be a hoarder to know what this attachment feels like, whether it's a favourite old sweater, a gift you've never used but can't bear to throw out, or every drawing your child ever did! Knowing that there is a biological basis to our irrational impulse to accumulate clutter is useful when it comes to overcoming the anxiety we associate with throwing stuff away.

And because we now know more about the science of addiction and how to rewire the brain, the good news is, whether you are an extreme hoarder or just an occasional stock-piler of junk, it is possible to change your habits.

The next few sections will start the process of deprogramming bad hoarding habits and forming healthier decluttering habits instead.

"WHETHER YOU ARE AN EXTREME HOARDER OR JUST AN OCCASIONAL STOCK-PILER OF JUNK, IT IS POSSIBLE TO CHANGE YOUR HABITS."

"CLEARING CLUTTER IS MAKING SPACE FOR HAPPINESS."

MAKING A START

IDENTIFY YOUR DECLUTTERING GOALS

So you've decided to sort your sh•t out - that's a fantastic
overall goal! But to stand any chance of actually making
it happen, you need to start breaking down your streamlined
dream life into manageable milestones.

Trying to overhaul everything at once can make you feel
overwhelmed before you've even begun. Indeed, the most crucial
step to successfully completing any major life project is to
first identify, and then clearly define, a series of smaller
goals in a very specific way.

GET MOTIVATED

Getting fully motivated will help you stay strong and stick to
your plans when the temptation to fall back into old patterns
inevitably appears.

Start by making a list of compelling reasons why you want
to stop hoarding. For example: "I want to be able to entertain
guests in my home" or "I want to be able to relax more after
a hard day at work". Review this list of motivations whenever
you start to wobble in your course of action.

1. ....

....

2. ....

....

3. ....

....

USE VISUALIZATION TO HELP ACHIEVE YOUR GOAL

One of the best life-coaching tools to help with goal setting is visualization. This popular technique simply means creating a vivid mental image of a goal you would like to accomplish in the future.

You set your mind to imagining a certain outcome in as much detail as possible, asking yourself leading questions such as, "What does it look like?" and "How do I feel when it's accomplished?" For instance, when it comes to decluttering your wardrobe, you might start by imagining rows of perfectly ordered shelves and colour-coded clothes rails. And you might also tap into the joy or pride and relief you might feel to be standing in front of them. Using these positive feelings as motivators to get you started is key.

FIND A QUIET PLACE

The first step in learning how to visualize is to find a quiet place to clear your mind and imagine your goals. You can choose your favourite spot in the house, a nice shady tree in the garden, or anywhere you know of where you can sit peacefully and not be disturbed. A quiet place is essential to having a good visualization experience.

CLEAR YOUR MIND

Once you have found the perfect spot, it's time to relax and clear your mind. When preparing for visualization, sit in a position that will remain comfortable for a while. Close your eyes and relax by taking a few deep, rhythmic breaths and clearing your mind of all thoughts.

If you have trouble emptying your mind, continue to focus on your breathing pattern, counting for five as you breathe in through the nose and slowly down from ten each time you breathe out. Repeat this process until you are fully present in the moment and your mind is empty. It can take a bit of practice, but stick with it.

IMAGINE YOUR GOALS

Now your mind is prepared, it's time to visualize those goals. In your mind's eye, imagine all the details of the final day of your project. Think about what you are looking at and who else is present. Think about what it feels like, even what you're wearing. Visualize as many small details as you can.

A good way to kick-start visualization is to ask yourself what's known as the "Magic Wand Question". If you had a magic wand, what would you transform - and what would the completed transformation look like? Don't worry about the practical reality or obstacles to be overcome. Use this process as an opportunity for you to think about what will really make you feel happy and satisfied when it comes to decluttering your life. Have fun with it and dream big!

Amassing clutter is a sign you're postponing life - try to live in the moment instead.

GET IT ON PAPER

While the future transformation is still fresh in your mind, write down below the five key ways your life will improve by learning to declutter and living a more minimalist lifestyle. Focus on the way you feel about yourself and your home. Be as specific as possible. The richer the details, the more meaningful and inspiring it will be.

1. ....
....
....

2. ....
....
....

3. ....
....
....

4. ....
....
....

5. ....
....

Fill out the following section, describing or sketching the
visual inside your head, or just making a note of the keywords
that describe your ideal for each room after you've decluttered.

	WHAT DOES IT LOOK LIKE?
LIVING ROOM	
KITCHEN	
BEDROOM	
BATHROOM	
HALLWAY	
CHILDREN'S ROOMS	
HOME OFFICE	
LOFT, CELLAR AND GARDEN	

DON'T TRY TO DO IT ALL AT ONCE

It's tempting to just go for it and try to blitz the whole house in one go. But not only will this impractical aim be exhausting and time consuming, a one-time blitz won't lead to lasting change when it comes to keeping clutter levels down. The secret to any success is breaking it down into baby steps that are easy to achieve - and repeating. For example, if you have a large, expansive goal like "Clean the whole house" it may even be hard to know when you've actually finished. And it could take so long your motivation may fade and you'll be back at square one in your mindset.

Instead, set a small, clear goal like "Clear the lounge bookshelf". With such a goal, it will be easy to know when you've completed it and the results will be very obvious, creating motivation and momentum for the next task. Alternatively, you can also set time-based goals, such as, "I will work for one hour each day to clear clutter."

ULTIMATE GOAL:

....

....

....

Three small, clear goals to work toward this:

1. ....

....

2. ....

....

3. ....

....

GET A STRATEGY

To rid yourself of current clutter and keep future clutter at bay, you need to develop a clear strategy for organizing things. One of the most common problems is deciding the actual value of an item - and then where it should live. So decide on how you plan to categorize the different items in your home, typically by item type or its common location - e.g. kitchen, living room.

In each space that you clear, designate a few simple piles, such as items to donate, items to sell, stuff to trash or recycle, or stuff to keep. Work on one area at a time until it's clear. Avoid just moving items from one area to another though, which brings us onto the next section of the book: your simple Sort Your Sh•t System.

" A ONE-TIME BLITZ WON'T LEAD TO LASTING CHANGE. "

YOUR SIMPLE SORT YOUR SH*T SYSTEM

In the next section of the book, you'll be going through each area of your house to be decluttered, room by room. To make the process simple, you need a system that's easy to apply to every item of clutter. The best way to approach this is to sort items into one of three categories:

1. KEEP IT:
I'm definitely keeping this item

2. BIN IT:
I'm definitely going to recycle or give away this item

3. UNDECIDED:
I'm not sure

When it comes to number 1, the Keep Its, set a simple rule that everything in it has to already have a place to go, a ready-made home for stuff you need and love.

The Bin It pile is also simple. You need to move it all out as soon as possible - bagging up stuff for the bin or to donate, making sure to recycle as many items and materials as you can.

The Undecided pile, however, will need further consideration. So get tough with your inner hoarder and ask yourself the following:

Does it make me happy?

Have I ever used it?

Will I ever use it?

Unless an item has future use and continues to bring joy, then it is probably a candidate for the discard pile. The aim is to quickly reduce your three piles to just two: Keep It and Bin It.

This foolproof system will also help you keep on top of future clutter. Just learning to distinguish between what you really need and use, rather than things you think you want, will limit some of the shopping and hoarding habits that led to this mess in the first place.

Have a bag ready for each pile so it can be easily and quickly transported to where it needs to go – whether that's a new permanent place in your home or the local second-hand shop. Having made some tough decisions, you'll want to make carrying out the actions as easy and as quick as possible to cut down any window to change your mind!

Now we'll look at some practical tips to make the physical sorting process more painless.

TRICKS TO MAKE IT EASIER

HAVE A "BELONGS IN ANOTHER ROOM" BIN

As well as having large bins or bags handy to put everything from your Bin It pile into, plus one for the recycling centre and one for donation, you also need a "belongs in another room" Keep It bin, for the stuff that's staying but moving to another part of the house. Then you can transport stuff easily from room to room - and put it away as soon as it's sorted.

ONLY SORT ITEMS ONCE

Avoid the tendency to put something to one side "until later" - as later rarely actually comes! Make your decision about each item you pick up straight away, ensuring you don't have to handle it again and again. If in doubt initially, use the undecided pile but once you turn your full attention to sorting through that pile, you need to once again make snappy decisions.

The best way to control your inner procrastinator is to only allow yourself 30 seconds to look at an item before deciding how to categorize it. These decisions can be hard but they're not complicated - and your first instinct will usually be the right one. Plus, the longer you ponder over an item, the more memories it will spark, the greater your attachment will become and the harder it will be to get rid of it.

Once you've decided an item's fate, place it in the correct pile - and don't go back or give yourself any chance to change your mind about it later.

"THESE DECISIONS CAN BE HARD BUT THEY'RE NOT COMPLICATED, AND YOUR FIRST INSTINCT WILL USUALLY BE THE RIGHT ONE."

DON'T BECOME DISTRACTED

You may be tempted to try to multi-task while you're having
a clear out - or even avoid the reality of what you're doing
by preoccupying yourself with other activities. But this is
a bad idea as you won't fully engage with the process of
decluttering and overcome your fear of doing it in the process.
There is a time to Instagram your life and this is not it! So
only focus on one task at a time and pick a time when you
won't be disturbed.

PICK A DECLUTTER SOUNDTRACK

Having the TV on in the background or chatting on the phone
is a no-no as it means you don't concentrate properly on the
task in hand. However, playing some of your favourite songs
is a good idea, as music can be very motivating and will make
the task more fun.

SET A TIME LIMIT

A full declutter is a marathon not a sprint - you need to
preserve energy for the long haul. Setting and sticking to
a limited time period can help keep you focused and ensure
you don't become too overwhelmed with the amount you have to
achieve. For example, decide to have a solid clearing out of
stuff for one hour, then take a break. Have a snack, go for a
10-minute stroll, or sit and meditate for a few moments. If
you then find you have enough energy to go again, you could
try a second hour.

MY PERFECT DELUTTERING PLAYLIST

1. ....

2. ....

3. ....

4. ....

5. ....

6. ....

7. ....

8. ....

9. ....

10. ....

TRACK YOUR PROGRESS

As you slowly move through your home room by room, keep track of the progress you've made, and how you feel about it, using a declutter journal. There's more detail on this journal in Section Three: Journalling Your Way Out of Clutter and Chaos. Making note of your progress can also help you gain confidence to deal with the remainder of your home. You might choose to take some "before and after" photos. Pictures are a great way to capture your achievements as you clear out each space.

REDUCE SENTIMENTAL STUFF BY 75 PER CENT

If you've always kept every childhood school report, every item of baby clothing, every love letter and holiday postcard, it's time to rationalize! Choose to save a few of the most special pieces and throw away the rest. You really don't need multiple versions of the same thing. If there is one particularly special item, such as a picture, then perhaps frame it and display it on the wall, where it will bring even more pleasure.

The same approach can be used to cut down children's artwork. Make it into a fun activity with your kids, ask them to choose a few favourite pieces with you and either display them or store them in a folder that will last.

And if you find it hard to throw sentimental items away, why not photograph each item and save to a special "memories" folder on your laptop or cloud storage first? You could even choose to display them on a digital photo frame. Then, not only are they stored safely, they will be seen more than ever, instead of being hidden away.

BOX IT UP FOR SIX MONTHS

If you simply cannot decide whether to keep an item or throw
it away, put it in a box for six months and store it somewhere
accessible in the cellar, garage or loft. At the same time,
make a note on your calendar of when the six months is up.
Then, when that date comes around, commit to dealing with this
problem item immediately.

The point of this exercise is that if you haven't opened the
box in all of that time, you can safely let it go without
regret. This is a great idea for people who hang onto items
such as old magazines, CDs, travel toiletries and other free
samples "just in case they come in handy".

GET HELP FROM A PROFESSIONAL

These days there's a raft of professional declutterers
available online and on local forums, who can help you clear
out your home if it's something you really can't face doing
alone. Even if you only book them for a day to help you get
started, having an objective person there with you while
you're clearing out your belongings can help make the process
easier. As well as lending a hand, a professional will give you
suggestions and advice, and will help you stay motivated to
finish the job.

The more things you
own, the more they begin
to own you.

HOARDING: WHEN EXCESS CLUTTER BECOMES A MORE WORRYING PROBLEM

We've all seen reality TV shows such as *Britain's Worst Hoarders* and watched aghast at people who can't get into their own bedroom at night - or even make a cup of tea in their own kitchen - due to mountains of clutter blocking all available space.

But when taken to extremeS, excessive hoarding is no laughing matter and can easily cross over into mental illness. Worrying hoarding behaviour is characterized by psychologists as a persistent and powerful difficulty in getting rid of large amounts of clutter, completely irrespective of its value.

Left untreated, hoarding can lead to damaging emotional, social, financial and even physical effects - for both the hoarder and their family members.

Being a serious hoarder can overtake your living space. For instance, you might have no chairs you can sit on as they're all piled up with stuff. Or you may not be able to access beds or the bathroom because of all the junk in them. As a result, hoarding can become the source of serious rows and high stress within families and can even break up marriages.

Overleaf are some of the telltale symptoms that indicate a clutter habit has morphed into a more dangerous problem of hoarding.

"LEFT UNTREATED, HOARDING CAN LEAD TO DAMAGING EMOTIONAL, SOCIAL, FINANCIAL AND EVEN PHYSICAL EFFECTS."

SEVEN SIGNS YOU HAVE A HOARDING PROBLEM

1. YOU GET VERY ANGRY IF SOMEONE ASKS YOU TO CLEAR YOUR MESS

If a family member or friends so much as suggest you have a clear out, do you find yourself reacting in an extreme, aggressive or overemotional way? Or do you avoid the issue completely by changing the subject? Maybe you react with dismissiveness or just leave the room. However you choose to deflect or avoid, the end result is that you refuse to get rid of any of your possessions, even if your behaviour is visibly upsetting loved ones.

2. YOU DON'T ORGANIZE YOUR STUFF IN ANY WAY

You might call yourself a "collector" but hoarding items is actually very different, so it's important to make the distinction between hoarding and collecting. Collectors are proud of their collections and enjoy organizing them, usually meticulously, and will often choose to display them. They tend to know where every item in their collection is, and are invested in maintaining things in good condition. Hoarders, on the other hand, are ashamed of their copious amounts of stuff and never get around to properly organizing their things, often choosing to hide them away or just piling them on top of one another around the house.

3. YOU HAVE A HOUSE FULL OF THINGS YOU SIMPLY DON'T NEED

Another telltale trait of a true hoarder is that you have huge amounts of items that serve no obvious purpose in your life, and seem useless or odd to others. This is also another thing which separates hoarding from collecting - hoarders will take and stockpile any old thing, from free leaflets to discounted sale clothes in the wrong size. These items aren't practical, they aren't for decoration or to complete a collection. Instead, it's the physical act of acquiring them and then hanging onto them that feeds the addictive impulse. The nature of the item itself is largely irrelevant.

4. IT'S BECOME IMPOSSIBLE TO CLEAN YOUR HOME PROPERLY

Are there areas in your house you can't get to and clean? Have they got very dusty or smelly, or even become damp and mouldy? Even if this is confined to just one or two spots in your home, it's an important sign that your accumulation of possessions is getting out of hand. Not being able to use any room for its intended purpose is another warning sign - bedrooms for sleeping, bathrooms for washing, kitchens for cooking, and so on. Indeed, if clutter makes a kitchen hard to clean, it can become a food hygiene issue and should be taken very seriously to avoid food poisoning.

5. YOU NEVER INVITE ANYONE ROUND TO YOUR HOUSE

When was the last time you had friends over? Many hoarders will find any number of reasons not to let people into their home, always choosing to meet up at other people's houses or in a café or park. This tends to be down to feelings of shame or embarrassment about their messy home and what others will think of them.

6. YOU'RE OVER-SENTIMENTAL ABOUT OBJECTS

We all have some personal items we keep from the past that we feel very strongly about - our first ever Valentine's card or the veil worn at our wedding, for example. But the emotions that hoarders feel about objects are different. They overvalue everything, not just the odd special item, and as a result become far too emotionally invested in their stuff and can't bear to let any piece of it go.

For example, you might feel you have to keep every train ticket you've ever bought or every Christmas card you've ever received. You fear that by throwing it away you will somehow lose the actual memory or experience too.

7. YOU HATE OTHER PEOPLE TOUCHING YOUR STUFF

Do you get angry if a friend or loved one tries to sort out your clutter? Usually the relationship a hoarder has with their stuff is a private one, which is very tied up in their feelings of over-attachment to what looks like useless junk to everybody else. This can make you react in an unreasonable way if someone wants to touch or tidy your stuff - or even just talk to you about it.

GETTING HELP WITH HOARDING

If you tick one or more of these criteria above, then launching into a full-scale clean-up of your home all at once is likely to be too emotionally distressing. You probably need to get to the root of your problem with hoarding first – and that usually means getting some professional help.

Experts recommend asking your doctor to refer you for Cognitive Behavioral Therapy (CBT) with a trained therapist. This talking therapy can help you understand the reasons why you hoard and, more importantly, how to improve the decision-making, organization and problem-solving skills you need to overcome it.

CBT sessions can be one-on-one with a therapist, or in a group setting. If possible, it's best to find a therapist who has worked with people with a hoarding problem before.

Sharing your experiences with other people who hoard may also help you feel less alone in this process, so look online for support groups. Talking to others in the same boat can help you learn different coping strategies for dealing with anxiety and means you can swap systems for controlling clutter.

Visit helpforhoarders.co.uk or hoardinguk.org for more help and advice, or search online for services local to you.

SECTION THREE

JOURNALLING YOUR WAY OUT OF CLUTTER AND CHAOS

While a journal can't actually cut down decluttering for you, keeping track of your progress can be an invaluable resource for changing your behaviour. As you let go of the past and embrace your new junk-free, more organized life, maintaining a journal of your journey will provide both motivation and momentum.

At first journalling might sound like being a teenager again and having homework. The key is not to see the writing as a chore but as a tool for empowerment.

The simple act of regular progress-reporting to yourself is one of the single best ways to break down your goals into manageable, bite-size chunks so the task in hand doesn't seem so overwhelming.

And journalling has other proven benefits too, with recent research showing that, practised regularly, it can reduce stress levels, boost mood and even lower blood pressure.

Either at the end of each day or as they occur, jotting down your thoughts and ideas helps you make sense of your overcrowded mind, relieve tension, and become a better problem solver.

Journal writing develops creative brain functions such as lateral problem-solving, intuition and emotional intelligence, as well as pragmatic brain functions such as rational thinking, order and logic. You will need to engage all of these strengths if you want to identify and overcome the challenges of living a clutter and waste-free life.

The very act of writing out our thoughts instantly calms the brain, providing it with the space it needs to focus on what you're actually doing at that very moment. Plus, consistent

"THE VERY ACT OF WRITING OUT OUR THOUGHTS INSTANTLY CALMS THE BRAIN, PROVIDING IT WITH THE SPACE IT NEEDS TO FOCUS ON WHAT YOU'RE ACTUALLY DOING AT THAT VERY MOMENT."

note-taking ensures you're not forgetting any of your ideas or to-dos.

In short, journalling provides a range of benefits – from tangible list-making to intangible mood-boosting – that will organize thoughts and ideas so we can put them into action.

The trick is to start small and not make journalling another chore. You don't have to spend more than 10 minutes making notes per day. And remember to have fun with it. Explore ways to make it a bit of secret "me" time. Try to find a time of day to do it when you have a little space to reflect in peace. Early evening after you've eaten is often a good time for this activity – you're not distracted by hunger, but you've not yet been taken over by sleepiness, which can happen if you leave journalling too late.

YOUR SEVEN-DAY GETTING STARTED JOURNAL

Ideally, start this journal on a Monday. No one feels like they have the energy to start changing their life on a Thursday or Friday when the week is winding down! The beginning of the week always carries that "fresh start" association, which will help spur you on.

Fill in your daily progress for the next seven days…

DAY 1

THREE THINGS I DID TODAY TO START MY DECLUTTER JOURNEY

These notes can be as modest and brief as you like - anything from "I sorted out the downstairs cupboard" to "I ordered a storage box from Amazon" or "I found a local shop where I can buy loose fruit and veg".

1. ....
....

2. ....
....

3. ....
....

THREE THINGS I'M PLANNING TO DO TOMORROW

Make these daily objectives realistic and achievable. Remember, it's all about the small wins at this stage. For example, clearing one shelf in the bathroom, or making a list of the local places you can take unwanted items to, such as second-hand shops and recycling centres, to ensure they're not just going to end up in landfill.

1. ....
....

2. ....
....

3. ....
....

DAY 2

TODAY'S PROGRESS. HOW DID EACH OF THE GOALS I SET
YESTERDAY GO?

1. ....
   ....

2. ....
   ....

3. ....
   ....
   ....

MOVING FORWARD: MY THREE GOALS FOR TOMORROW

1. ....
   ....

2. ....
   ....

3. ....
   ....
   ....

DAY 3

TODAY'S PROGRESS. HOW DID EACH OF THE GOALS I SET
YESTERDAY GO?

1. ....

   ....

2. ....

   ....

3. ....

   ....

   ....

MOVING FORWARD: MY THREE GOALS FOR TOMORROW

1. ....

   ....

2. ....

   ....

3. ....

   ....

   ....

DAY 4

TODAY'S PROGRESS. HOW DID EACH OF THE GOALS I SET
YESTERDAY GO?

1. ....

....

2. ....

....

3. ....

....

....

MOVING FORWARD: MY THREE GOALS FOR TOMORROW

1. ....

....

2. ....

....

3. ....

....

....

DAY 5

TODAY'S PROGRESS. HOW DID EACH OF THE GOALS I SET
YESTERDAY GO?

1. ....

....

2. ....

....

3. ....

....

....

MOVING FORWARD: MY THREE GOALS FOR TOMORROW

1. ....

....

2. ....

....

3. ....

....

....

DAY 6

TODAY'S PROGRESS. HOW DID EACH OF THE GOALS I SET
YESTERDAY GO?

1. ....

....

2. ....

....

3. ....

....

....

MOVING FORWARD: MY THREE GOALS FOR TOMORROW

1. ....

....

2. ....

....

3. ....

....

....

DAY 7

TODAY'S PROGRESS. HOW DID EACH OF THE GOALS I SET
YESTERDAY GO?

1. ....

....

2. ....

....

3. ....

....

....

MOVING FORWARD: MY THREE GOALS FOR TOMORROW

1. ....

....

2. ....

....

3. ....

....

....

MY SEVEN-DAY RECAP:

It's important to continually check in with how you're doing and identify what's working and what isn't.

Write down your three biggest achievements this week. The three tasks that you're really proud to have put behind you, whether it's finally recycling the enormous pile of newspapers sitting in your hallways or spending an hour decluttering your pantry. Take the time to also note down how each accomplishment made you feel? Happier? Less stressed? In control? Productive?

1. ....

....

....

....

....

2. ....

....

....

3. ....

KEEPING IT GOING

Journalling in this way will help you get started and,
provided it becomes an easy and useful part of your daily
routine, it's a good idea to keep the journal going for the
entire time you're decluttering your home. If you do hit any
speed bumps in your journey, the journal will help keep you
motivated and on track.

YOUR
ROOM-BY-ROOM
DECLUTTERING GUIDE

Now you have the Sort Your Sh*t system in place for tackling
clutter, and your journal at hand to record your progress, it's
time for action!

In this section we will work our way through every room in
the house - cupboard by cupboard, drawer by drawer - removing
all the junk that's serving no purpose other than to clutter
your home and clog up your life.

We will systematically work through which items you want to
keep and which you can bin or donate - because, let's face it,
we all accumulate needless things on an almost daily basis.

Just ask yourself:

* How many spices in your kitchen pantry have never
been used or are past their use-by-date?

* Do you really believe you'll ever find all the lids
for your Tupperware collection so it can be used again?

* What about those odd socks, or clothes that no
longer fit?

It's time to wave goodbye to unnecessary mess and clutter once
and for all.

Read on to clear your living spaces and move toward a calmer,
happier life in the process

LIVING ROOM

The living room is one of the hardest rooms in your home to keep neat on a daily basis. That's because while it generally gets a lot of use, your average lounge doesn't contain a huge amount in the way of storage options. You may have some bookcases and a TV cabinet, but they don't hide much, which means remotes and blankets are often left hanging around. Keeping your living room surfaces clear is essential for an inviting space, so clutter containment is key.

When you're trying to decide which items to keep in your living room and which to store elsewhere, think of what you really do in that space and keep only things that you will frequently use there. And remember, even if you technically have room for something, it doesn't mean that you should automatically keep it! Learning to relax with less is about stripping back to only the essentials.

GETTING STARTED

Remember your Sort Your Sh•t system. Sort everything into three piles:

1. <u>KEEP IT</u>

2. <u>BIN IT</u>

3. <u>UNDECIDED</u>

SORT SOME SPACE

If you don't have them, create permanent storage spaces
for commonly used items such as books and Internet routers.
Floating shelving is ideal.

BE A BASKET CASE

Invest in a set of pretty storage baskets - they're great
for holding extra blankets, keeping magazines or tidying up
kids' toys.

BOX CLEVER

Decorative boxes are perfect for storing necessities such as
remotes, while a pretty tray works well on a coffee table to
both display your favourite objects and make moving them out
of the way easier.

STREAMLINE OBJECTS ON DISPLAY

If you're a collector at heart, you can quickly end up with
lots of trinkets covering every shelf of the living room.
Commit to the belief that less is more when it comes to
ornaments. Pick one or two items you really love, which make
you happy when you look at them - and consign everything
else to the donation box. This will ensure your favourite
pieces have their chance to shine, plus, from a practical
perspective, you'll find it much easier to regularly clean a
clutter-free shelf or surface.

CLEAR OUT YOUR CUPBOARDS

Once you've done the surface decluttering, it's time to dig a little deeper. Start with bookcases, cupboards and side tables. Empty them, assess the items they store, then return them to their proper storage spaces. Have a bag handy for any rubbish. Put books away, action any post and return remote controls to their proper places. Then go through drawers looking for any items that you don't love or need – be prepared to find lots of random objects that were tucked out of sight a long time ago!

CUT BACK ON DISCS

Increasingly, we live in an age of streaming media, from music to movies. So take a long look at any shelves or cupboards full of CDs or DVDs. This may include some old favourites that you're proud to display, but ask yourself: is a disc even how you play them anymore? With technology continuing to move toward cloud storage and streaming, you can clear lots of valuable space by decluttering all your old media.

MOVE ONTO ELECTRONICS

Remove everything that's not connected to your current television or music system. Are you using it? Does it work? Even as we upgrade our entertainment equipment, it's amazing how we still hang onto old cables, chargers and remote controls. Store the add-on items you do need, such as computer gaming controls, in the cupboard closest to your screen.

QUESTION THAT MAGAZINE RACK

These are secret clutter collectors! Although they signal good intentions of being tidy, when you take a closer look, they are always full of out-of-date magazines, old post and other junk. Do you really need one? If not, ditch or donate it! And perhaps rationalize your regular reading material, too - if a new issue of a magazine arrives and you still haven't read the last issue, perhaps it's time to unsubscribe.

EXERCISE EQUIPMENT

You might think sticking an exercise bike in front of the TV is a great idea to get you working out, but unless you're actually going to use it regularly, it just ends up being an eyesore or a place to dry clothes! While it's vital to look after your health, a treadmill, rowing machine or cross trainer shouldn't be in the living room if at all possible. Is there an area in a spare room, garage or garden room where it could go instead?

CUSHION CULL

We get it - there are some gorgeous, colourful cushions out there, and the magpie in you yearns to gather up all these pretty things and take them home. But too many cushions all over your living room can quickly become clutter, not to mention impractical. As a rule of thumb, if you need to move them all before you can actually sit down, you have too many! Try halving the amount.

PAPERWORK PILE PURGE

The living room should be a place to put your feet up,
but piles of paperwork there just remind us of all the
unfinished stuff we still have to do. Instead, create a
holding section in your kitchen or hall for all incoming
paperwork and set a weekly time to action it. Avoid touching
it until you're actually ready to deal with it - that
way, you won't keep moving it around the house until it's
impossible to find!

WASHING OR IRONING?

Much like paperwork, having piles of laundry stacked
everywhere is simply a reminder of all that's left to be done.
Unless you're actually about to iron, the living room is not
the place for piles of ironing to live. Ditto the ironing board
and iron themselves.

TACKLE THOSE TOYS

Every parent has stepped on bits of plastic before. And
hearing battery powered toys suddenly chirp or burst into
song of an evening is not relaxing! First of all, make sure
your children have sufficient toy storage in their bedrooms.
Realistically, some toys may need to be stored in the living
room but that doesn't mean they have to be visible once the
kids are in bed.

Buy an attractive toy chest or easy pull-out baskets for
existing cupboards, then go through and assess every toy for
wear and tear, asking: Does it still work? Do the kids still
play with it? Then bin, donate or store away each toy.

TACKLE YOUR "BELONGS IN ANOTHER ROOM" BIN

Lastly, you're not finished in this room until you've returned everything that belongs elsewhere in the house to its proper storage space. Don't leave anything lingering in the bin!

KEEP UP THE GOOD WORK

* Declutter your lounge regularly. For young children, incorporate "tidy-up time" into their evening routine, make playing with toys contingent on them later putting the same toys away in designated boxes.

* Think carefully next time you buy furniture. Too much will make even tidy living rooms look cluttered. If you have a small home, don't choose large, bulky furniture, particularly dining tables and sofas. If we can afford the space then this isn't a problem, but many of us can't!

* Think about buying smaller, more streamlined furniture such as tables that can fold away or fold out to become bigger. Also, "double-duty" furniture with storage incorporated, such as ottoman coffee tables or footstools, have items like blankets stored inside them, which is great. And do you really need that four-seater sofa, or will a smaller one look prettier and save on space?

BEFORE

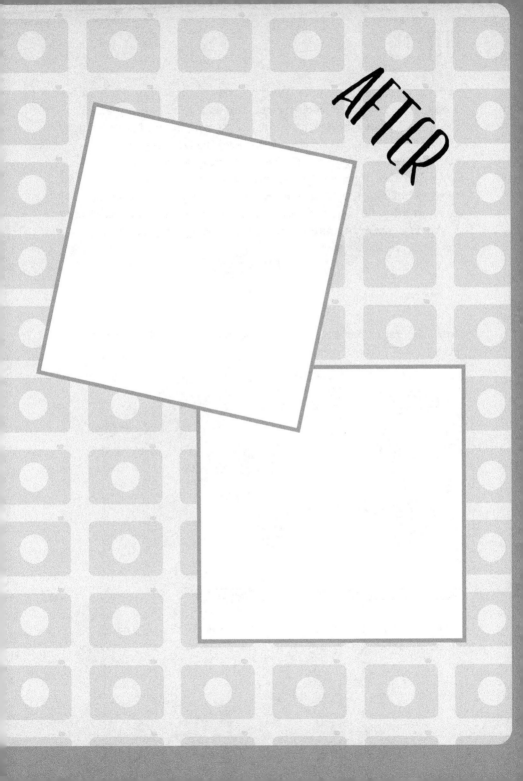

AFTER

KITCHEN

For many of us, the kitchen has become the heart of the home – a centre not just for cooking but for eating and entertaining, too. This new style of open-plan living and socializing brings many advantages, but it does make keeping your kitchen clutter-free a bigger challenge. This single space will have many different types of items stored within it, not least because, unlike the living room, which tends to be lacking in drawers and shelves, the kitchen is nothing but storage. This makes it a powerful magnet for unused gadgets, gizmos and junk – so let's get sorting!

GETTING STARTED

Remember your Sort Your Sh*t system. Sort everything into three piles:

1. KEEP IT

2. BIN IT

3. UNDECIDED

CONCENTRATE ON YOUR COUNTERTOPS

Move as many items as possible off the countertops and into storage spaces. Only keep on the surfaces what you use every single day. This will leave you more room to actually prepare food, which will encourage you to cook more often!

GET INTO THOSE CUPBOARDS

The first step is to completely empty each space, assessing every item as above, then put everything back where it belongs. Start with your biggest storage spaces first, such as the pantry and upper cabinets. Then move onto the lower cabinets, drawers and the space under the kitchen sink.

Your kitchen cupboards might be full of mismatched china, unused utensils and even that cheese fondue set you were gifted, to name just a few of the common items we hang onto. Get rid of anything that's damaged, neglected or unpleasant to use. Again, less is more. You need trusted, quality kitchen tools that are fun to use and easy to find!

When it comes to foodstuffs, ditch anything past its sell-by date, unwanted gifts, or foods you know you will never eat. Donate anything reusable. Bin the rest, putting actual food out for food waste collection whenever you can.

BE RUTHLESS

It may be tempting to hang onto objects in case you need them "someday", but that's not a valid reason to hoard stained, mismatched Tupperware or a cracked serving bowl. For every 20 things you give up, there's a small chance you may end up regretting one. Save the space for something you're using now.

Donate storage containers without matching lids, dishes you no longer use and cookie cutters collecting dust to free up valuable room in your cupboards. Get rid of any sets of crockery that don't have at least four place settings. Do the same with mismatched cups and mugs or anything chipped.

Now take a long hard look at those kitchen gadgets and appliances - the ones that sounded so amazing, but you've barely or never used. Donate or sell any of these space sucking items. We all know secretly that "someday" will never come!

EASY ACCESS

Once you've pared down these items, streamline your kitchen to enhance the experience of making and eating a meal. Creating "zones" by grouping similar items together allows you to see everything you own and makes finding your cooking essentials a breeze. And think about frequency of use. Anything you use on an almost daily basis should be easily accessible obviously. Store medium-frequency use items such as cake tins and extra-large saucepans on mid-height shelves or cupboards. Rarely used appliances such as pasta machines and ice cream makers - but only if you actually use them! - can go in those hardest-to-reach top cabinets; otherwise they should be donated.

THINK VERTICALLY

Do you just stack saucepans and baking trays in any old jumble? Try applying some logic and order instead. Stand stationery file dividers in deep drawers to create a nifty way to vertically line up items such as trays, baking sheets

and lids. (IKEA makes good file dividers.) And always stack
your mixing bowls, pots and pans and china in size order.
When storing your best china, place a sheet of kitchen towel
between each piece to help prevent any chips or breakage
caused by friction.

FIT SOME SPACE SAVERS

Install some pullout drawers to maximize space in pantries
and lower cabinets – you can get them from Amazon. You can
also add freestanding corner shelves (try Lakeland.co.uk) to
existing cupboards to make sure no space is wasted.

MAKE OVER YOUR PANTRY

One of the quickest and simplest ways to make your pantry
look neat and tidy is to transfer food items into matching
jars. Items such as flour, cereal, seeds, nuts, rice, pasta and
dried fruits look Instagram-ready displayed in glass Kilner
jars. Group foodstuffs together and label the jars in large
print so you know at a glance what they contain. Keep all
your spices on one shelf, then all your baking items on
another.

PUT NON-KITCHEN STUFF AWAY

Lastly, you're not finished in this room until you've returned
everything that belongs elsewhere in the house to its proper
storage space. Just because the kitchen has lots of drawers
doesn't mean they need to be filled with non-kitchen junk! If
you are determined to keep it but it doesn't belong with food
and cooking stuff, move it to another room now.

DECLUTTER YOUR FRIDGE AND FREEZER

It's surprising how much clutter can accumulate in a fridge freezer, but the good news is, it doesn't take long to sort it out.

Start by removing everything from your fridge and cleaning inside thoroughly with a sponge and hot soapy water. Pull out drawers and wash thoroughly in the sink. Then throw away all food past its best, all condiments past their use-by date or unused because you didn't like them. Again, put actual food into a food waste bin for collection by your local authority, if they provide this service.

Now it's time to put things back. If your refrigerator shelves are adjustable, take a moment to plan what you want to go where and place them accordingly. As you replace each item, be sure it's clean. Wipe off any sticky containers or lids.

Store like things together, with meat always on the bottom shelf (so any juices don't drip onto other food) and fruit and veg in the lower drawers. Dairy such as milk and butter can go on the upper shelves or in door storage shelves. Keep raw and cooked food separate and have an area just for leftovers if there's space.

When it comes to the freezer, you might want to consider a full defrost to clean it thoroughly and start again. Too much build-up of ice and frost creates clutter on its own. As for food, get ruthless and remove anything that's over three months old or that you know you don't actually like. Despite your good intentions at the time, if you have frozen leftovers that you haven't touched in a month, you're unlikely to use them ever. Repeat this clear out once a fortnight to keep your freezer clean and clutter free with limited effort.

" **THE STATE OF YOUR FRIDGE CAN REVEAL A LOT ABOUT YOUR STATE OF MIND, GIVING THEM BOTH A GOOD CLEAR OUT IS LIFE-ENHANCING!** "

COULD KITCHEN CLUTTER MAKE YOU UNHEALTHY?

According to recent research into eating habits the answer could be Yes. A Cornell University study in 2016 suggested that the stress triggered by your clutter may also trigger coping mechanisms such as overeating comfort foods. Meanwhile, another psychological experiment conducted at the University of Minnesota noted similar results, finding that a messy room was more likely to lead to eating unhealthy snacks than healthy ones. In fact, people who spent time in a chaotic room were twice as likely to eat a chocolate bar than an apple! While there may be multiple reasons why people eat poorly in cluttered surroundings, it certainly makes sense to make cooking and dining areas as free of clutter as possible - especially if you're trying to eat more mindfully and prepare more meals yourself.

KEEP UP THE GOOD WORK

After every meal put all the cooking items and equipment back where they belong. If someone in your household typically does most of the cooking, make clearing a task for the non-cook. And don't allow post or other non-kitchen clutter to stack up on work surfaces or the kitchen table. Mark a date in your calendar six months ahead for a cupboard purge, and ditch anything not used since the last one. Finally, plan your meals for the week ahead, making a note of what ingredients you already have and what you need to buy.

	MEAL	INGREDIENTS IN STOCK	INGREDIENTS TO BUY
SUNDAY			
SATURDAY			
FRIDAY			
THURSDAY			
WEDNESDAY			
TUESDAY			
MONDAY			

BEFORE

AFTER

BEDROOM

To be properly restful your bedroom should be an oasis of calm, not a scene of constant chaos. This means the number of possessions stored there should be low and unobtrusive. Yet it's all too common for bedrooms to become a general dumping ground for laundry, unpacked bags, beauty products, books and other random items. Because it's generally not a room visitors see, it's often the last place you get around to clearing, even when other rooms get a quick tidy. But in truth, decluttering the place where you sleep every night should be one of your top priorities. Read on to turn your bedroom from a messy storeroom into a peaceful sanctuary.

GETTING STARTED

Since an unmade bed can make the whole room feel messy, get in the habit of making it every morning for a bit of instant order. A simple, all-season duvet is the easiest to smooth out if you want to get the job done quickly. After the bed is made, glance around as if you're a visitor and this is your first time in the space. Notice the first things that stand out, then think about what needs to change - what can stay and what really needs to go?

Now, remember your Sort Your Sh•t system. Sort everything in the bedroom, including clothes, into the three piles. With each one, ask yourself: Does it serve me well? Is it broken? Do I use it?

1. KEEP IT

2. BIN IT

3. UNDECIDED

"DECLUTTERING THE PLACE WHERE YOU SLEEP EVERY NIGHT SHOULD BE ONE OF YOUR TOP PRIORITIES."

TACKLE YOUR BEDSIDE TABLES

This is a spot where all sorts of junk typically accumulates. Remove anything from the surface that shouldn't be there and put it in your "belongs elsewhere" bin. This may include books you've already finished reading, used paper, post you need to answer and cups you need to wash. Throw out or recycle anything you no longer use, such as empty tissue boxes, pens that have gone dry or phone chargers that no longer work. Do the same with the tops of your chests of drawers and blanket boxes. Pay careful attention to any clothing strewn about. Anything that needs folding or hanging goes into the "to be put away" pile.

DRESSING TABLE DRESS-DOWN

Sort out all that beauty clutter. Be ruthless, only keeping items you've used in the last week or so on the top. Things you have used recently, but don't need daily, can go into drawers. Resist the urge to just shove things back into drawers without careful consideration. Instead, bin or recycle any rubbish or items you haven't used in more than six months.

JEWELLERY BLITZ

Spend some time putting earrings into pairs, untangling twisted items and binning anything broken or missing its twin. If you don't already have one, invest in a decent jewellery box that's big enough to fit your whole collection. Choose a multi-layered box and make sure it has separate pull-out sections for earrings, necklaces, bracelets and rings. If you can see all of your collection just by opening up the box, you won't need to get everything out each time you're looking for the piece you want to wear. Now get into the habit of putting any items worn that day back in their spot each night.

ITEMS I'VE NOT USED IN THE LAST SIX MONTHS

1. ....

2. ....

3. ....

4. ....

5. ....

6. ....

7. ....

8. ....

9. ....

10. ....

11. ....

BE RUTHLESS WITH ORNAMENTS

If you've been hanging onto old presents, family "treasures" or ugly trinkets solely out of guilt, now is the time to stop. If you don't love them and they don't make you smile, give them away. Your goal is to make your home clutter free and comfortable for you. Remember, your affection and love for the person who gave you these objects doesn't change just because you let go of their gifts.

KEEP UP THE GOOD WORK

Make a promise to yourself to put your clothes away immediately, whether it's clean laundry or your office outfit at the end of a work day. By taking the time to put your things where they belong, you'll keep the space tidy and keep your clothes looking good for longer. You'll also be less likely to buy new items just because you can't find what you need.

As soon as you've read a book or magazine, shelve it, recycle it, give it to a friend or donate it to charity. This will ensure that the pile by the side of your bed doesn't start getting too big again.

HOW DECLUTTERING CAN IMPROVE YOUR SLEEP

Keeping your bedroom tidy and ordered is a great way
to target insomnia, as when a relaxing space is filled
with clutter, it can subconsciously disrupt your
sleep. This is because our brain interprets mess as a
task that needs to be completed, making us feel anxious
and alert when surrounded by it, so it's harder to switch
off and get into the calm, wind-down mode we need to
enter in order to drop off.

Part of this good sleep hygiene also includes
keeping electronic devices turned off all night.
Smartphones and tablets emit a blue light that works
to shut off your brain's production of melatonin,
the hormone that makes you feel drowsy and tells
your body that it's time to sleep. To give your body's
melatonin production plenty of opportunity to kick in,
you need to switch off all screens at least an hour
before bed. Experts also recommend storing them outside
your bedroom, where they can't disturb you or be a
distracting temptation if you're struggling to sleep.

STREAMLINE YOUR WARDROBE

Okay, take a deep breath. It's time to tackle your wardrobe – and any clothes stuffed into chests of drawers or below the bed while we're at it!

A **proper clothing cull requires a slightly different approach** to decluttering elsewhere. Probably the easiest way to approach this sort out is to work by type. That means starting with shoes, then boots, then dresses, then denim and so on.

It's much easier to decide to toss or keep a pair of jeans if you're looking at your entire jean collection all at once. So start pulling out different types of clothing and decide what you'll toss and keep.

Try them on in front of a mirror right now, and ask yourself honestly:

* Does this look nice?

* Does it fit okay?

* Do I feel good wearing it?

* Can I see myself wearing it again soon?

If you answer Yes to all these questions, it stays – if you get a No, it's bye-bye time!

Anything that's too big or too small, worn out or full of holes, or badly stained has no place in your wardrobe. Similarly, if it's just too hard to find something to match an item, then it's not worth keeping. It may be pretty but if it is difficult to wear - for example, because it creases badly - then that is a definite maybe.

Think about whether you really have the occasion to wear favourite old pieces anymore. As our lifestyles and body shapes alter with age, our wardrobe should change, too.

Be ruthless and recycle shoes you don't like or that have fallen out of fashion, even if you've never worn them. And get rid of any shoes that hurt, no matter how expensive they were -you won't ever wear them and you need the space more than an option you never take.

Finally, look at the items you have multiples of and narrow this down - for example, if you have six "useful" white T-shirts, get rid of any that are greying or have lost their shape slightly.

Once you've gone through each type of clothing, you'll have four piles to deal with:

1. Dirty laundry - put it in the laundry basket straight away.

2. Anything that needs to be repaired or dry cleaned - put in a bag by the front door to take to the tailor or dry cleaner ASAP.

3. Clothes to donate or sell.

4. Items you want to keep.

THIRTY IS THE MAGIC NUMBER

Decluttering professionals say you should really aim to
minimize your clothes to 20-30 items. This carefully curated
capsule wardrobe should contain all your everyday essentials,
plus a few special outfits.

FOUR IS THE FLOOR FOR SHOES

If you drill down to absolute basics you really only need four
pairs of shoes: smart heels, smart flats, casual lace-ups and
boots. Get into the mindset that everything else is extra. Of
course, you'll probably keep more pairs than that, but make sure
each extra pair really earns their space. This could be because
they offer a practical alternative (for example, trainers if you
like running) or just a pair you are truly passionate about.
Anything that brings real joy you should keep, of course.

CREATE A HOLIDAY BOX

Realistically, in many parts of the world there aren't many
days a year when it's sunny enough to wear bikinis, strappy
dresses, kaftans and sandals, so having them permanently clog
up a sizeable portion of your wardrobe just doesn't make sense.
Get a box just for true summer gear and store it up high out
of season. Likewise with cold-weather gear.

STORE SPECIAL OCCASION STUFF

As with holiday clothes, special occasion garments can be
stored away from your everyday wardrobe - after all, a ball
gown or wedding hat takes up a significant amount of room,

and probably only gets worn once a year at most. Pack them away carefully using acid-free tissue paper to keep them in perfect condition. And make sure the box is clearly labelled so you know exactly what's in there before putting it away on a high-up shelf or above a wardrobe.

PROTECT YOUR CLOTHES

One of the joys of creating a clutter-free wardrobe is that you can actually take care of and protect your clothes properly. Once you've done your clear out, clean the entire inside of the wardrobe or chest of drawers, ideally using natural cleaning products. Next, add in some form of moth protection – hanging sachets are a good option for wardrobes, and can be bought easily from Amazon. Avoid wire hangers as they can ruin the shape of clothes. Opt instead for skinny, wooden hangers which don't take up too much room.

STOP SEEING WARDROBES AS HIDING PLACES

You don't put clothes in a wardrobe just to get them out of sight. You need to think of your wardrobe as an organizing tool. At a minimum, this means hanging clothes by type – for example trousers, skirts, jackets, dresses. To go one step further, order the colours from light to dark.

Another expert tip is to turn all the hangers the wrong way around, so the hooks face you. Then, the first time you wear each item, you can turn the hook the right way. After six months, any items not turned the right way have never been worn, which makes them prime candidates to donate or sell.

MAXIMIZE YOUR HANGING SPACE

Install some double rails in your wardrobe with the lower
one hanging about halfway down, so it's perfect for hanging
shirts, skirts and other shorter items. You don't even need
to install them - just look for the type that hooks onto your
existing rail. Shelf dividers will prevent piles of sweaters
from collapsing and are great for organizing handbags
and scarves.

FEET FIRST

Finally, a good shoe system will help keep everything off
the floor, whether you prefer clear shoe boxes, an over-the-
door rack, or traditional wardrobe-floor shoe racks.

CREATING YOUR DREAM LINEN CUPBOARD

A perfectly ordered linen cupboard, filled with neat shelves
of towels and bedding, is a thing of beauty. To get yours
in order - and keep it that way - place everyday towels,
sheets and other linens at the front and centre so you don't
have to disturb everything when you need to get them out.
Store infrequently used items, such as beach towels, holiday
tablecloths and out-of-season blankets, on harder-to-reach,
upper shelves.

A great way to avoid sorting through individual bed sheets
every time you need a clean set, is to store sets in bundles.
Make a bundle by folding the undersheet and duvet cover and
all but one pillowcase together, then tucking the all these
folded items inside the remaining pillowcase to make a tidy
pack. Simple!

KEEP UP THE GOOD WORK

Make sure you don't let your wardrobe get out of hand again. Part of living a clutter-free lifestyle is committing to shopping less and sadly, that has to include clothes! To make sure you only buy things you need or really love, start a "one in, one out" wardrobe policy. This will ensure that everything you add truly deserves its place in your clutter-free space.

Do a seasonal detox. As the seasons change, so too do your wardrobe needs. At the start of every new season take a few moments to review this season's capsule wardrobe. Eliminate anything that no longer fits, or perhaps just feels like last year's style, and move any out-of-season garments to the harder-to-reach areas.

BEFORE

AFTER

BATHROOM

While the bathroom might not be the most obvious room to amass clutter, its many drawers and cabinets can house all manner of half-forgotten products. There's the treatments tried once then set aside, the bottles with just a squeeze of shampoo left, various pills from past illnesses - and much more besides. In fact, a woman uses an average of 12 beauty products per day - from shampoo to mascara - according to figures from the US Environmental Working Group.

Twelve may sound like a lot, but how many do you actually have stored in your bathroom cabinets? Fifty? Sixty? More? If you're a habitual hoarder of beauty buys then it's time for a product amnesty to clear out all that clutter because living the simple life really is more beautiful in the long run.

GETTING STARTED

Implement your Sort Your Sh•t system. Sort everything in your bathroom into three piles:

1. KEEP IT

2. BIN IT

3. UNDECIDED

START WITH YOUR BATHROOM CABINETS

Take everything out and discard outdated medications,
kids' bath toys that have gone black and mouldy, make-up
and skincare products past their best, plus anything you
haven't used at all in the last year. Recycle any plastic
you can. Unused prescription medication should be properly
disposed of at a pharmacy. Unopened toiletries can often be
donated to a charity or a women's shelter.

SORT THE REST IN PILES AND GIVE THE CABINET A

GOOD CLEAN

Next, put everything you're definitely keeping – apart from any
medicines, which we'll come to next – immediately back into the
cabinet. Store the items you use the most often, such as tooth-
brushes, contact lens solution and face wash, at eye level. Only
store a few rolls of toilet paper in the bathroom itself – the
rest can live in the linen cupboard or cellar to save on space.

KEEP MEDICINE SAFE

Although we commonly store them in the bathroom, it's actually
a much better idea to move medication and first-aid items
elsewhere. They're not suited to the steamy atmosphere of a
bathroom and can spoil and become damp quickly. You're better
off keeping medicine in a linen cupboard, kitchen cupboard
or other cool, dry place. Organize all the items into separate
open, holding boxes – IKEA make great ones – grouping them by
illness. For example, cold and flu, tummy troubles, pain relief,
hay fever and so on. Then store on a high cupboard shelf, well
out of reach of children and pets.

CLEAR THE LEDGES

Follow the same clear and clean routine around the bath and shower, only allowing one or two everyday-use items to return there. All the others must be binned or given away if not used, or put into cabinets or drawers if they're used but less frequently.

SINK SAVER

Use a glass mason jar or similar to store both your toothbrush and multiple make-up brushes to help neaten up the area around your sink.

FIND A GOOD TOWEL SOLUTION

Add hooks to the back of doors or to walls to keep in-use towels hung tidily, and have a basket under the sink to store clean towels.

KEEP UP THE GOOD WORK

Don't take the mini toiletries from hotels or accept cosmetic samples from department stores unless you know you'll definitely use them. The reality is most of us never get around to using them and they just end up taking up needless space in our cupboards and drawers.

Drawers are often one of the biggest disaster zones in a bathroom as everything is a mess inside, so pick up some drawer dividers from your local stationery shop or home store to add instant order.

BEFORE

AFTER

HALLWAY

Your home's main entrance is obviously one of the highest-traffic areas and even small hallways can quickly turn into a dumping ground for discarded shoes, junk mail and goodness knows what else if you let it. But remember, it's the first area other people see when entering your house and can therefore set the tone for the rest of the property. Just as important, it's the first area you see every time you come home, potentially giving it a disproportionate effect on your own mood, so it's critical it always looks clutter free and calm.

CLEAR THE CONSOLE TABLE

A hallway table is the place where everything gets discarded and dumped upon entering the house - indeed, it gets cluttered so quickly, it usually needs a daily purge. To get started, go through all the items on the top, making a quick decision on whether to bin or keep each one. Then go through each drawer, removing the contents and doing the same. The hall tends to pick up a lot of clutter from other rooms, so spend some time putting away things from elsewhere that have made their way there.

CREATE A DROP SPOT FOR DAILY ESSENTIALS

Having a dedicated space for your keys, sunglasses or handbag will save you from searching for misplaced items every morning. Use a pretty tray or small wooden box to store these important items in. This reliable resting spot will make your mornings easier, while still keeping the hall table looking tidy.

SORT JACKETS AND SHOES

Do you really need all those jackets or shoe options by the door? If your winter coat is still hanging up in summer or your flip flops are still around in autumn, then it's time to put them away. Only your most frequently used coats and shoes should be on display in the hall. If you don't already have a better place to store spare coats and shoes, then think about adding a dedicated cupboard. Speaking of which...

TAMING CUPBOARD CHAOS

If you do have a hall coat-cupboard, then it needs regular decluttering just like any other wardrobe. Just because it's hidden away doesn't mean it needs to hoard unseasonal styles, as I mentioned earlier. Start with shoes and boots, then jackets, followed by accessories. Keep, donate or bin any items you don't love or need.

THINK ABOUT A GETTING A SHOE CUPBOARD

Having somewhere to put away shoes and boots is one of the single biggest ways to make a difference to the feel of your hallway. Having no footwear left out immediately makes the space feel tidier and more welcoming. IKEA does great, simple shoe cupboards, or if you can't find one the right size for your space, think about getting a local carpenter to create a bespoke one for you. It shouldn't cost too much, provided you shop around and get a couple of different quotes.

HOW DECLUTTERING HELPS FENG SHUI YOUR HALLWAY

Feng shui is an ancient Chinese practice that has gained huge popularity in recent years as a holistic way of organizing your home layout. The basic principle is that our homes are a mirror of what's happening inside us, and therefore we should aim to get our surroundings in alignment with who we really are and where we want to go. In other words, you harmonize your energy with your home's own energy.

According to the principles of feng shui, to create a harmonious home you need to ensure there is good energy flow - known as chi - in every room. This is done by carefully considering everything you bring in, how you arrange your rooms and how you maintain order there. For feng shui advocates everything has its own chi, even inanimate objects. Feng shui helps guide that energy and lets it flow freely through your home.

The front door and hallway of a house is called "the mouth of chi" in feng shui and it's believed that this entrance determines the overall fortune and happiness of those within it. When a house has enough good chi coming into it and its flow is calm and uninterrupted, the people living in the house are said to experience a greater sense of well-being and contentment. Because of this, decluttering your hall and keeping it clear and chaos free is thought to be very beneficial.

KEEP UP THE GOOD WORK

To ensure your hall stays clutter free, sort your post
as soon as it arrives, before putting it down. That
means immediately opening anything that could be
important and recycling any junk mail. And remember to
implement the "paperwork pile purge" method mentioned
on p114.

Make decluttering a regular thing. No matter how small
your hall, the best way to keep it organized is to have
a declutter once a week. Try setting a time - such as
every Sunday morning - to blitz it for 10 minutes.

SIX WAYS TO CREATE SOME CALM

1. ALLOW ENERGY TO FLOW FREELY

According to feng shui, the front of a staircase should not face the doorway. If this happens the flow of energy into the home will be funnelled up the staircase, preventing energy from moving through the rest of the space. If you already have a staircase facing your front door, placing a large plant or sculpture at the bottom of it can slow the escape of energy.

2. PUT UP MIRRORS AND PAINTINGS

A wall opposite the front door is thought to block the flow of energy into the home. Your first instinct might tell you to hang a mirror there to open the space, but this is thought in feng shui to bounce the energy straight back out of the house. Instead, place a landscape picture facing the doorway. This helps attract the eye, gives the space depth and creates the illusion that there is a view beyond the wall.

Mirrors are still great accessories in a hall, especially if it is small, narrow or dark. Place them on walls on either side of the main doorway, at a height that reflects the light, to make the hall feel larger.

3. LET THERE BE LIGHT

Speaking of light, the more your hallway gets, the better it will feel. Lots of light helps create a bright and airy feeling upon entering your home. If your space lacks natural light, find the brightest light fixture possible. You might even consider placing extra uplighters on your walls to boost brightness.

4. PICK YOUR PALETTE CAREFULLY

Repainting your hall in a different shade is another easy way to make it more feng shui friendly. Painting your front door a shade of red is thought to attract positive energy, while black is said to draw wealth to you. A dark, closed-in hall should be painted in a light shade to brighten the mood and lift energy levels.

5. BOOST ENERGY WITH CRYSTALS

In Chinese folklore it's thought that crystals amplify positive energy, so they're often used in feng shui to improve the feel of a home. If your front door lies at the end of a long hallway, all of the energy is thought to rush into your home. Placing a crystal over the door will help calm this energy and create a more balanced flow.

6. KEEP IT CLUTTER FREE

The hall provides a transition from the outside world to the inside world. Clutter is seen as stopping energy from flowing and can have a psychologically negative effect, so it's important that energy coming into your home is unobstructed. Yet one more reason to keep it clean and well organized!

BEFORE

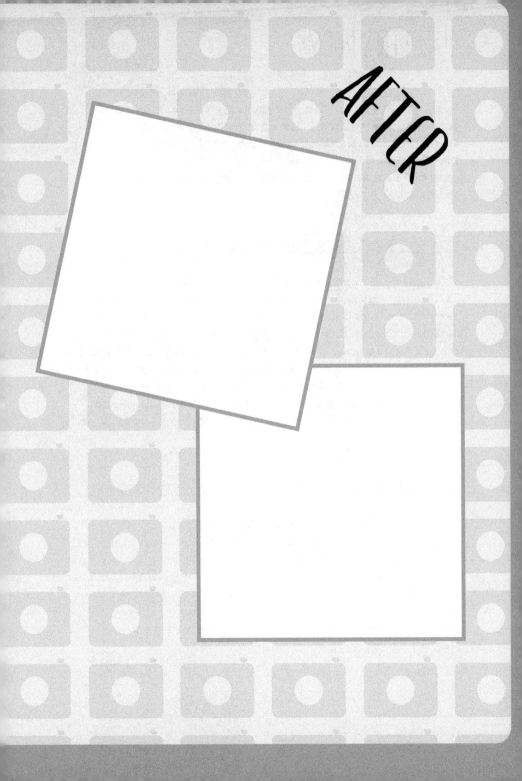

AFTER

CHILDREN'S ROOMS

If there's one room you wish you could lock the door on and never look at again, it's probably your child's room! Thanks to the endless piles of toys, books, clothes and crafts in rotation at any one time, keeping this area clutter free can feel like an impossible and endless task. Here are some tricks that can help make the transformation - and maintenance - easier.

INVOLVE KIDS FROM THE START

Although your first instinct might be to wait until your children are at nursery or school so you can throw stuff away without complaint, getting your kids to help with a declutter is actually a really good idea. You might think they'll find it boring, but in reality most find it fun and will want to have a say in how their toys are organized. Involving them from the outset will also give them some ownership over the project, so they'll be more inclined to keep things tidier - or at the very least, they'll know where everything should go!

GET THEM TO GIVE YOU A TOUR OF THEIR FAVOURITE STUFF

It's not worth asking kids to choose what should stay or go - they will inevitably refuse to part with even the smallest piece of tat. Instead, ask them to show you around their room, pointing out to you their favourite bits and why. This will give you a good sense of which things are most important to them, and what could perhaps now be safely donated to younger children via family or a second-hand shop.

EXPLAIN HOW ALL STUFF HAS A HOME

Do you remember your parents telling you as a child to "put all that junk away" when your room was messy? This is actually a pretty negative way of expressing a wish for tidiness, but with a simple language tweak you can easily reframe this task in a more positive light. Younger children have a natural affinity for personalizing toys and other objects, so saying things such as "Where do we want this to live?" or "Shall we find this toy a nice home?" makes sense to them and better captures their imagination, so they will be keener to help.

GIVE THEM PERMISSION TO DITCH STUFF THEY DON'T WANT

Too much stuff can actually be overwhelming for kids, but they also don't know how to say No or give up things they no longer need. Give them the chance to sort out a pile of toys they no longer play with "to help some children who don't have many toys". The idea that their toys are getting a new home feels much more positive and like doing something good, as opposed to just getting rid of stuff for the sake of it.

MAKE IT A GAME

If possible try to make clearing up feel like play. Ask your child to collect six items to put back in their "homes" at the end of the day, and time them as they do it, offering a reward for taking less than two minutes, for example. This feels more manageable than just "tidy everything up" and can help reinforce the habit of daily tidies.

BE A NEAT FREAK

Kids mirror what their parents are doing and even something as small as putting away your shoes, jacket and keys every time you get home acts as a lesson in action. Tidy parents equals tidy kids, so lead by example!

USE YOUR SORT YOUR SH*T SYSTEM

Sort everything into three piles:

1. KEEP IT

2. BIN IT

3. UNDECIDED

PUT ART ON THE WALL

Clear out the desk drawers by neatly framing some of your child's best art masterpieces and hanging them in their bedroom.

TOY BASKETS AND BINS

Store toys and stuffed animals in their own baskets, but
remember: the deeper the storage container, the harder it is to
find something and the easier it is for the mess to start up
again, so don't buy huge ones.

THINK ABOUT BOOKS

Instead of storing books on traditional bookcases, stand them
upright in a shallow bin or storage basket. A child can easily
flip through and pull out a favourite, but more importantly,
it's a lot easier for little fingers to replace books in a bin
than back on a shelf.

HANG BASKETS

Another way to clear floor space is by hanging baskets from
the ceiling to be filled with anything that needs a home –
crayons or Lego, for instance.

BOX THINGS UP UNDER THE BED

Spare bedding, out-of-season clothes and old toys they won't
let go of just yet can live boxed-up under the bed. You can buy
canvas or wooden boxes to fit under most bed heights to help
utilize every bit of space available.

RUN SHELVING AROUND THE ROOM

If you've used up all the cupboard, box and chest space in the room, then try adding a discreet shelf around it. This space is perfect for storing cuddly toys when children are young and photo frames as they get older.

CUPBOARDS IN CORNERS

Just because your child's room has an awkward corner or sloped eaves doesn't mean the edges are out of bounds. Fixing a made-to-measure cupboard into these areas creates more room to store items your little hoarder can't bear to part with.

TACKLE YOUR "BELONGS IN ANOTHER ROOM" BIN

Lastly, remember you're not finished in this room until you've returned everything that belongs elsewhere around the house to its proper storage space straight away. Don't leave anything lingering in the bin!

A calmer space means calmer kids - and that's something we all want!

KEEP UP THE GOOD WORK

Designate mini clean-up times. It's always easier to get the kids onboard to help if there are only a few items they need to put away.

Children like to do fun things fast, so clean up regularly rather than leaving it until it looks like a bomb went off in their playroom, leaving both you and your kids feeling overwhelmed. Ten minutes tidy-up time after dinner each night is a manageable amount, and by doing a little and often, you should avoid needing to spend another whole day blitzing the area.

HOME OFFICE

Working from home can be great, but work can also be yet another source of clutter for your home. Even if your work is mostly waste free, all too often a home office becomes another place for the junk of everyday living to pile up. Whether it's a dedicated office or a corner of your kitchen or bedroom, your computer desk really needs to be a clear work surface for you to work at your best. The good news is a small home office should be one of the easiest areas to declutter and get super organized, which can really help boost your productivity.

GETTING STARTED

Use your Sort Your Sh•t System. Sort everything into three piles:

1. KEEP IT

2. BIN IT

3. UNDECIDED

PRIORITIZE WHAT'S KEPT OUT

Keep frequently used office products close at hand, but store extra printer paper, rarely used reference books and office supplies, like toner cartridges, in drawers. Only keep your printer within easy reach if you use it at least weekly. Prevent cords, wires and cables from taking over by using a cable organizer, available at office supply or home stores.

STREAMLINE YOUR LIBRARY

Home offices are often packed with books and binders of paper, which are rarely, if ever, consulted. Check to see if any of your hard copies are available online so you can ditch them. And if you're holding on to something you haven't opened in years, consign it to the recycling.

SORT YOUR STATIONERY

Gather items such as pens, file folders and other office supplies into categories and assess what you truly use and need. Keep the stuff you use daily on top, and move secondary supplies (scissors, paper clips, rubber bands, etc.) to a drawer. For added convenience, it's a good idea to line any drawer with the kind of organizer insert that can be found at stationery shops.

PARE DOWN PAPER

Paper can soon pile up, so make sure to print out only the things you need a physical copy of. Recycle any papers you don't need and keep on top of your paperwork with an organized system that provides a proper place for everything. File any paperwork you must keep but also consider digitally scanning documents to instantly cut down all that paper clutter.

TACKLE YOUR "BELONGS IN ANOTHER ROOM" BIN

Lastly, you're not finished in this room until you've returned everything that belongs elsewhere to its proper storage space. A home office should not be another dumping ground for clothes!

KEEP UP THE GOOD WORK

Sort your ins and outs. Once your desk is clear, add two file boxes or trays to it. Designate one box for incoming projects and papers and the second for items that need to be posted or returned.

Get into the habit of clearing your desk at the end of every day to keep clutter from accumulating. It's also a good way to signify to your brain that work is over for the day, so you don't keep returning to do more - a common problem for home workers.

BEFORE

AFTER

LOFT

The loft is traditionally a place of holding - a space for long-term storage of all those items not needed in the rest of the house, or maybe things needed once a year, such as Christmas decorations. The problem is, the loft is so "out of sight, out of mind" that it's all too easy to forget about everything that lives there, adding more and more to it as time passes and never really thinking about what's up there, let alone needing it again. When you finally need to declutter properly, perhaps as part of a house move, you will have an enormous task on your hands.

Do you want to tackle your loft but don't know where to start? Read on for a guide to a stress-free declutter of your loft space.

DO A LOFT AUDIT

Some lofts can appear very well organized with items neatly stored in stackable plastic boxes. Other lofts, meanwhile, are full to the brim with random bags and piles of indiscernible junk. But the truth is, tidy or untidy, if we're honest, most of us can't actually remember everything that's up there!

So logically, your first step is to identify what you have stored and start to create groups of similar items, like seasonal decorations, holiday stuff, sports equipment, memory boxes, DIY equipment, camping gear, old baby stuff and so on. Depending on the headroom in your loft space, you may need to bring the items out of the loft to do this properly.

Once things are organized then it's time for a purge, asking yourself:

☐ Do I use it?

☐ Would I save it in a fire?

☐ Would I buy it now?

☐ Does it make me happy?

Store items you love in a memory box. But then make tough choices about the rest - ask yourself, will you even notice if it's gone? Which brings us on to the next question...

☐ Do I actually need to store anything?

Before you go any further, don't assume that you need to store anything at all in the loft. In fact, it could be a whole lot better for you, both mentally and physically, to have an empty space above your head rather than to feel the pressure of lots of clutter weighing down on you. An untidy loft could be draining your energy without you even realizing it. Of course, there are some things you do want to store in a dry space for longer periods (no point buying new tinsel every year!) but it certainly pays to be very strict with yourself about what you will allow up into the loft. Make a list and stick to it!

Use the following suggestions as a guide and write down a list of things you do want to store:

* Suitcases

* Christmas decorations

* Memory boxes of old cards, letters, etc.

* Occasional-use items such as ski wear and sports kit.

* Camping gear.

Now make a list of all the things you're not going to store. Good examples of things you should put on this list are:

* Boxes of old clothes or books that you've decluttered from other rooms in the house but haven't yet parted from properly. Take them and donate to a second-hand shop – now!

* Every possible memento of your child's education from nursery until university. Save just the key reports and school books – and ditch the rest. Can you remember the last time you looked at all your old school stuff? Exactly!

* Old furniture, cushions, curtains – sell or donate them. If they are in the loft, it's surely a sign you'll never use them again.

* Anything broken – because if you had any intention of fixing it, it wouldn't even be up here!

* Anything that you couldn't remember was up there - the fact it was forgotten means you have absolutely no need for it.

* Empty boxes. Because whyever would you keep them? Recycle now!

* Excess luggage. Have you invested in new suitcases but for some reason still kept the old ones? They should be donated to charity straight away. You only need one set of luggage.

* Family "treasures". If you've hung onto any items you have no love or use for just because you feel guilty ditching them, then they should go, too! Would your family member rather they were hidden in a loft or get the chance to be used by someone who actually likes them?

ONLY PLAN TO SELL STUFF YOU CAN BE BOTHERED TO

We all love the idea of finding cash in the attic, but be realistic. Are you ever going to get around to sorting and selling the valuable stuff? And how much money will you actually make? Only save stuff to sell if you truly intend to do so - and then set yourself a timeframe of one week to either list it on eBay or take it to a car boot sale.

GET SNAP HAPPY

Many of us store items such as clothes and other mementos in the loft as we really don't want to part them, but what good are they up there if you never get to look at them? Instead of hiding them away, why not take photos of them and create a keepsake photo album that you can easily store in a bookcase in your home, which you can open whenever you want to reminisce. Then donate the actual items themselves.

SORT AND STORE IT WELL

Once you've grouped similar items together and purged unwanted items you can start to put the things you want to keep back in the loft and organize the space by theme. Think about how you can make more of the space you have available – can you swap to stackable boxes or even add in extra shelving? The items that you need to use more frequently should be stored nearest the access door. All boxes should be clearly labelled, ideally with photos on top of them showing what's inside.

FIVE TIPS FOR STORING DELICATE ITEMS SAFELY IN YOUR LOFT

There's nothing worse than storing stuff in the loft only to find it's damaged when you return to it later. Here's how to ensure more vulnerable items stay in good nick.

* Soft toys – can attract dust mites and mice, so always store in airtight plastic containers.

* Carpets and rugs – very attractive to moths, so get them cleaned, then spray with moth repellent before bagging in plastic.

* Old photographs and pictures – can be affected by temperature, light and damp, so store in waterproof containers away from light and heat.

* Vintage clothes – can be damaged by excessive light, dampness and moths, so they need to be cleaned first, then kept in airtight plastic.

* Books – prone to damp and silverfish (a type of insect), so store in airtight containers.

KEEP UP THE GOOD WORK

Next time you think about putting something up in the loft, refer to your list of what's actually allowed in there - if the name's not down, it's not getting in! To avoid your now pretty clear loft filling back up too quickly, operate a "one in, one out" policy to further limit what makes its way up there.

CELLAR

Whether you dream of turning your basement into a more usable home space, or it's where your washing machine currently lives and you're tired of facing an overwhelming mess every time you go to do the laundry, the cellar space is one area that needs a thorough sort out in most homes.

Much like the loft, basement spaces are also prone to becoming a dumping ground for all those things that you're not yet ready to get rid of, but don't really love - or need. And because it's literally beneath your feet, the cellar is often the last space in your home to be decluttered, so let's not delay it any longer!

As with every other room in the house, the same rules apply - if you haven't used it or don't really value it, donate it to someone who will or find a way to recycle it.

CAN YOU REALLY SELL IT?

As with lofts, many of us keep heaps of stuff in the cellar that we have a vague plan for selling. But years later we still have a pile of boxes and no cash! Again, be sensible when hanging onto items - think about how much time you will need to put into selling versus your return. Flog any high-ticket items and donate the rest to charity. You'll feel so much better for letting them go!

SHOULD IT STAY OR GO?

Cellars are usually a bit more accessible than loft spaces but can also be pretty damp, which makes them unsuitable for many items.

Using the examples below as a guide only, make a list of all the items in your home that can happily live in the cellar:

* Household supplies, bulk-buy toilet paper, laundry liquid and other similar items.

* Half-full paint cans – only keep colours that are actually on your wall, so you have them handy for touch up purposes.

* Extra dining chairs, used when guests come, and leaves that extend tables.

* DIY toolboxes and items like light bulbs, which you don't use often but might need to grab quickly.

ITEMS BEST KEPT OUT

As with any other space, ditch anything broken or unwanted but do remember that cellars can be damp, so unless your basement space is particularly dry, try to avoid anything that can warp, mould or mildew, for example:

* Letters, magazines, photos and other paperwork

* Mattresses, pillows and cushions

* Furniture and other wooden items, especially untreated wood

* Cardboard boxes.

DESIGNATE DIFFERENT ZONES

Now it's time to create a storage plan. Think of all the things you found in your cellar during the decluttering phase and create some distinct zones, perhaps according to activity or season. This will help keep the clutter and chaos under control and make it easier to find stored items when you need them. Make large, clear labels for each area and start piling things up by each label.

INSTALL SOME SHELVING

If at all possible, never store anything directly in contact with the cellar floor, where damp can creep in. It's a good idea to get some sturdy shelving in place, which will allow air to circulate, while also enabling you to see exactly what you have stored.

ELIMINATE TOOLBOXES WITH A WALL STORAGE SYSTEM

Plastic containers and shelves are ideal for items you're looking to store in the cellar, but what about the ones you use more regularly? If you keep your DIY tools in the cellar, having easy access to them needs to be high on the priority list. One way to achieve this is to create a system for hanging them on a wall. This can be done easily by using various hook sizes, or getting a pegboard - have a look on Pinterest for ideas and then pop into your local DIY store for supplies

UPGRADE YOUR LAUNDRY AREA

If you have your washing machine and tumble dryer in the cellar, there are lots of things you'll want to store to go along with them, such as detergent and clothes baskets. Installing a cupboard - freestanding or fixed - can help organize messy laundry items so they're out of sight but easily accessed. This in turn will improve the look and functionality of your space.

A few simple organization tricks can make going to the cellar less like a scene from a horror movie - and just like any other room in your home!

MAKING THE CELLAR A LESS DAMP SPACE

Most cellars will always be damp, which makes storing anything a risk. However, there are some simple steps that can help reduce some of the dampness:

* Scrub the walls and floor with detergent and water, followed by a rinse with a diluted household bleach solution.

* When the walls and floors are dry, paint everything with an anti-mould and waterproofing primer.

* Consider using a heavy-duty waterproof paint for the floor, on top of the primer, as it will act as an additional sealant against moisture.

KEEP UP THE GOOD WORK

Make it pretty - even if it's just the place you store toilet rolls or wash clothes, the prettier a space is, the more likely you are to keep it clean and organized long-term. So put in the effort to make things nicer by painting the walls, hanging a couple of pictures and adding some decent lighting.

Do a yearly inventory - now that you've gone through a lot of effort to sort your cellar, make sure it stays that way. Once a year, review exactly what's in there and get rid of items that are no longer needed. Kick the habit of continually adding new things without sorting through the ones you already have.

BEFORE

AFTER

GARDEN

Gardens are an extension of our homes, places to relax and enjoy ourselves when the weather is good. However, just as happens inside the house, pretty much every horizontal surface - be it tables, decking or even the garden path - can end up becoming a magnet for all those items that never quite made it back into the house, garage or potting shed. And unfortunately, these things have a way of becoming "invisible" to us the longer they remain in place.

Whether it's a bicycle lying on the lawn, a hose abandoned in a flower bed or a child's broken swing, outdoor spaces can just as easily become cluttered with life's debris as our indoor spaces.

The good news is one of the quickest ways to improve the appearance of any garden is to spend a weekend decluttering it. By doing so, you'll be creating space to give things you love - such as all the beautiful plants and flowers - room to breathe, and maintaining an outdoor oasis that you and your loved ones can enjoy.

GETTING STARTED

Choose a time slot when you'll be able to devote a stretch of several hours to your yard work, such as a weekend morning, and gather together your equipment. Here are some suggestions of bits you might need:

* Thick protective gloves for handling broken glass and prickly plants.

* A wheelbarrow.

* Extra-large, strong bin bags.

* Garden tools, such as a leaf blower, rake, pruning shears, shovel, trowel.

START AT THE FRONT

The front garden is part of your property's kerb appeal so pay special attention to it, especially if your home is prone to litter blowing in from the street.

GET A SYSTEM

Set up simple storage systems now to make it easy to keep things organized in the future. For example, the easiest place to store large bins is close to the street, concealed if you can by a wooden roof or hedge. Designate a spot for the bins, so that putting them away in the future takes absolute minimal effort.

MAKE IT PRETTY WITH SOME QUICK WINS

In the spring and summer months, it's easy to make your garden look its best by just adding a few hanging baskets and pots of colourful plants. You don't need to be a good gardener to put a few things in pots and the difference it makes to your space can be dramatic. If you have more money to spend, you could buy new garden furniture or maybe upcycle the furniture you already have as a winter outside will cause wear and tear.

SORT YOUR SHED OUTSIDE

If you have a shed, make sure it is neat and tidy, with doors and locks working and woodwork painted and treated for all weathers. You could also try making a shed a feature of interest instead of just a functional building by painting it a pretty pastel colour, or in coloured stripes for a trendy beach hut effect.

AND INSIDE

Just like cellars and loft spaces, sheds are notorious clutter magnets - much of which is likely to be rubbish. So be prepared to get your hands dirty, brush away some interesting cobwebs and make several trips to your local recycling centre or dump.

Organize everything you decide to keep in your shed in wooden storage boxes, labelling them just as you would in indoor storage spaces. Most home stores and garden centres offer good shed storage systems to help you stay organized, but very regular-use items are better kept out loose for ease of use.

Sort through all the garden tools and repair or recycle broken ones. Keep usable tools in good shape by cleaning them, then put them away neatly. Try eBay or websites such as Freecycle to find new homes for items that are still useful, but you no longer want.

When you stop treating the shed as just a dumping ground, it suddenly becomes a useful, working space.

DON'T FORGET THE GARAGE!

Be honest, can you actually get your car into yours?! If not, you're far from alone - one in four people say they can't to squeeze their car into its rightful home thanks to too much clutter, according to research.

Even if you don't have a car, or are happy using your garage as an extra storage space, it still has to be organized to be useful. This means the area still needs decluttering and ordering - and for you to stop thinking of it as a dumping ground.

The first step of a garage clear out is to gather everything together that can be binned and box or bag it up to be taken to the tip. Then gather everything that can be donated to a good home and do the same. Finally, you'll be left with all the things you actually want to keep. Now is the time to get them in piles according to type, ready to be tucked away in their rightful places.

A well-organized garage should be divided into areas dedicated to specific tasks and themes - for example tools, bikes, sports equipment, garden furniture and lawn care. Arrange it so that frequently used items are easily accessible, while seasonal ones such as sledges and beach chairs are placed in a separate storage area that's harder to reach. Maximize vertical space on the garage walls with some sturdy shelving systems for larger items.

EXCESS PLANT POTS

It's surprisingly easy for empty plant pots to end up dotted around the garden, so now is the time to sort them. Pick up any clay pots you're not currently using and get them inside before they're cracked by winter's cold. Are you saving the thin plastic pots that nursery plants came in, hoping you'll find a use for them? Cut the clutter by freecycling or recycling them.

OUTGROWN OUTDOOR TOYS

Once your kids are older, it's time to get rid of those outdoor swing sets, climbing frames and water slides, all of which take up substantial space in your garden. Not to mention all those balls and rackets and plastic garden games. Anything that's still in good enough shape can go to a good home - perhaps even to someone on your street.

OVERHAUL GATES AND FENCES

As part of your garden blitz, check fences and gates. A decayed or shaky rail or post is an accident waiting to happen. Get them replaced. Then oil any squeaky gates and ensure that all woodwork has been treated or painted with a protective coating to increase its lifespan.

HOSE IT DOWN

Everything looks better when it's been cleaned. There are lots of specialist cleaning materials and tools available to get patios, decking and furniture looking all sparkly and new once more.

Borrow a jet-wash (from a friend or they are available to hire online for a reasonable cost) and blast the algae and slime from your decking and garden path. Not only will an annual clean improve the way they look, it will stop them becoming dangerously slippery in the winter months.

WEED IT OUT

Weeds are unsightly and ruin the look of an otherwise pretty garden. On top of this, these unwanted plants tend to be incredibly hardy, fast-growing and space-hogging, so the sooner you deal with them the better. Stop weeds before they push out the grass, flowers or vegetables you do want to grow and thrive.

TIDY YOUR BEDS

Remove any plants that don't work, or that you just dislike, to make space for new ones. Give live plants to neighbours or friends. Compost dead plants, unless they're diseased. In that case burn or bag them so they won't infect future plants.

Take the time to assess plants that have been underperforming, replacing fruit trees that produce poorly and getting rid of any plants that look sickly. Perhaps it's time to heavily prune an older tree to open up a view of the sky?

DEAL WITH DANGER

Tackle sick trees or those with broken or low-hanging branches. An unsound tree or limb – whether dead, damaged or diseased – poses a danger to people, animals, plants and

property. Trimming branches can be a DIY project, but larger
jobs such as tree removal should be tackled by a trained
tree surgeon for safety.

FIND OUT WHERE TO DISPOSE OF GARDEN WASTE

For all the stuff you can't repurpose, get clued up on what
your local council will collect. Most councils will provide
you with a separate garden bin or bag for this purpose.
Alternatively, you can take garden refuse to your local
recycling centre. Some debris can be incinerated on a home
bonfire, but do check the council website for any guidelines,
while a home composter will eventually turn both garden
and food waste into useful fertilizer.

REINVENT YOUR GARDEN STYLE

Take advantage of all that new-found space to rethink your
plan for how you want your garden to look, what plants would
work in the future, a new furniture arrangement and the
overall feeling you would like to create.

A gorgeous garden is
hiding under all that
clutter – it's time to help
it emerge.

KEEP UP THE GOOD WORK

Embrace "less is more"

A successful garden is a relaxing haven to de-stress in. Keeping it this way means keeping the clutter to a minimum, enjoying open, empty spaces and resisting the temptation to fill them up. Before acquiring new plants or accessories, think about whether they will add beauty and joy to your garden – or just more junk.

Respect your remaining stuff

The best way to avoid constantly acquiring new tools, furniture and plants is to take better care of the ones you already have. Treat possessions with respect, which means cleaning tools, sharpening blades, storing summer furniture in the winter months, and watering and feeding plants. You don't have to be an expert, you just need to show living things some love and attention.

WORK

If you've spent time decluttering your mind and house, the last thing you want is to leave your home on weekdays and enter a cluttered, chaotic space at your place of work. We can spend at least 40-50 hours a week at work, so it makes sense to take some time to clear and sort your sh•t out there too.

It doesn't have to take long - just a few simple changes to your workspace and you could be lowering your stress and boosting your productivity. In fact, sorting sh•t at work should empower you to keep better track of meeting notes, project plans and generally be more effective. And since you've already mastered decluttering your home life, you'll be familiar with all the tidy mindset tricks you need to create the perfect working environment.

Here's how to get started...

PICK YOUR MUST-HAVES

The thought of sorting your workspace can be a bit overwhelming at first, so you need to start by identifying the necessities. Which items do you need every day to do your job? Keep these within handy reach. Everything else should go directly to the office recycling points or be tidied into a drawer. This first step will keep you organized and focused on the task at hand.

ZONE YOUR DESK

One way to help smarten up your desk and boost your work performance is to assign your various work tasks to different areas on your desk. "Zoning" in this way can help you compartmentalize and prioritize your work better. It also helps streamline your work flow throughout the day, helping you to mentally shift as you physically shift from task to task.

The zones will depend entirely on the type of work you do but examples of distinct zones include:

* Researching zone

* Writing zone

* Meeting zone.

DON'T USE YOUR DESK AS A DINNER TABLE

Even if you bring your own lunch to the office, eating it at your desk as you work is one bad habit worth breaking. Not only will this immediately reduce clutter and crumbs, but getting up and away from your desk at lunchtimes will also help manage stress and boost your energy levels.

Research shows that employees who take a break from their desks during the day feel they come back with renewed energy and creativity for the tasks at hand. By planning the day well, everyone can afford at least half an hour away from their desk to eat lunch. Plus, diet research has found that we are more likely to overeat and make unhealthy food choices if we do eat in front of a computer screen, so you'll be looking after your health into the bargain.

So declutter your desk of unnecessary plates, forks, food containers and snacks, and take your lunch outside or to a communal indoor food area. Just anywhere but your desk!

BIN AND HIT DELETE

One of the best ways to declutter and get organized in your workspace is to free it from needless paper, as well as unnecessary digital clutter such as unwanted emails. Which means you need to clear up and recycle paper, and at the same time do a full digital detox of your inbox.

Assume everything can be thrown away or deleted, unless you can come up with a very good reason to keep it! The aim is to create a calm environment that not only helps you feel less cluttered, but actually enables you to become more organized in your habits going forward. There will be less junk to sift through and more time to focus on the actual task you want to complete – or that deadline you need to meet.

KEEP IT CLEAN

Your office may have cleaners but chances are they've never been able to see all of your desk before! So give your desk a really thorough clean after you've sorted it all out. Use a natural disinfectant spray to remove germs and dirt. Clean your keyboard and computer monitor with a special screen cleaner and cloth. This final clean will help you maintain the good work.

WORK DECLUTTER CHECKLIST

☐ IDENTIFY THE NECESSITIES. WHAT ITEMS DO YOU NEED TO DO YOUR JOB?

....

....

☐ ZONE YOUR DESK. WHAT ZONES DO YOU NEED TO BE MORE ORGANIZED?

....

....

☐ PLAN YOUR DAY AND MAKE TIME FOR LUNCH. WHAT WILL ENABLE YOU TO TAKE 30 MINUTES AWAY?

....

....

☐ GET RID OF NEEDLESS PAPER, CLEAN YOUR DESK, COMPUTER SCREEN, KEYBOARD, DRAWERS, THE LOT!

....

....

STAYING CLUTTER FREE

FOUR HACKS TO STAY CLUTTER FREE

Now you've come to the end of your decluttering journey and blitzed every area of your life, you need a few ground rules to help ensure it doesn't get a chance to build up again.

ADOPT A "ONE IN, ONE OUT" POLICY

You can't live a streamlined life if you're not also a responsible consumer. It's especially important these days, as we're more mindful of the impact our shopping habits have on the environment. The good news is if you buy only what you need from now on, you'll never be faced with a mammoth decluttering effort again!

A good rule of thumb, to be an ethical consumer and keep a lid on future clutter, is that for every new item that you buy, you have to responsibly get rid of one you already have - either through donation or recycling, so you're not just adding to landfill waste. Every new pair of shoes acquired means giving away an old pair; every paperback you buy means donating to a friend one you've already read.

DON'T DELAY, DO IT TODAY

Procrastination is the precursor of clutter, so try not to put off small tasks for later. Sort out your post the minute it lands on the mat instead of letting it pile up. And set aside a five-minute daily blitz of new rubbish rather than let it get out of hand.

ENLIST THE HELP OF FRIENDS AND FAMILY

Family and friends can be a great source of encouragement as you attempt to maintain control of your clutter. Ask them to help ensure you don't restart any hoarding behaviours by reminding you of the reasons you wanted to live clutter free in the first place.

To help you make better decisions, arm them with the same set of questions you've used throughout this book:

* Why are you holding onto this?

* Is it useful?

* Do you love it?

BECOME THE HOST WITH THE MOST

Make the most of your clear home by throwing regular parties, or if that's a bit much for you, a series of smaller social gatherings with one or two friends. For example, offer to host a book club at your place once a month, or simply have a close friend or relative to stay regularly.

Having a more open-house policy like this can be a very effective way of ensuring that your accumulation of clutter doesn't get out of control again. If you know that someone is due to visit every couple of weeks, the fear of social embarrassment can work in your favour as it will mean you're far less likely to let any mess pile up again.

THE LIBERATION OF LIVING WITH LESS

Now that your home and head are both feeling a lot less cluttered, it should be more apparent that too much baggage, whether physical or emotional, holds us back from pursuing the life we want. Through the simple act of creating space, we can bring a greater sense of calm and happiness. Learning to live with less helps us to focus on the important stuff in life, such as positive relationships and fun experiences.

While the advertising world would have us believe that we need to consume more stuff to be happy, for most of us the opposite is true. Once you make the conscious decision to own less stuff, you automatically stop seeking out new items to bring into your home. It's just a given. Which also means you'll be spending less as well. The money you save can be spent on better-quality items that last longer, again cutting down on unnecessary buying.

For example, choosing classic style staples over fast fashion means that you won't throw away clothes after a single season. And of course, in a world polluted by the waste of excessive consumption, changing your personal habits has real benefits for the environment, too. Keeping and buying less will also help you to treasure and take better care of the things you do decide to hold onto. You will have successfully created more space for them in your home and in your heart.

RESPONSIBLE CONSUMPTION: FIVE WAYS
TO MAINTAIN A SIMPLER LIFESTYLE WITH LESS

* Don't treat shopping as a leisure activity. Only go when you need something and always take a list with you when you do go. Stick to what's on the list and leave without getting distracted.

* Always look for used items before buying new ones. Check secondhand shops, eBay and car boot sales. When it comes to items that you only need to use once or twice a year – for example, a carpet steamer or a leaf blower – try to borrow from family and friends first. Or you could even decide to purchase a shared occasional item with family or friends. It's also getting easier to hire many items online.

* If you do buy new, save up and get something higher-quality that will last longer than the cheaper versions on the market.

* Scouring second-hand shops or having style swapping parties with friends are great ways to update your wardrobe at little or no cost. But try to remember your "one in, one out" rule – sell or donate to create room for something new to love.

* Try to buy multipurpose gadgets where you can, such as a slow cooker that's also a pressure cooker and a rice cooker. The more uses an individual item has, the fewer additional gadgets you'll need. Investing in a bit of extra research could save you money and space here, too.

NOTES

NOTES

NOTES

NOTES

NOTES

NOTES

NOTES

NOTES

NOTES

NOTES

INDEX

CPSIA information can be obtained
at www.ICGtesting.com
Printed in the USA
JSHW040230110921
18604JS00004B/4